THE LIFE IN CHRIST

NICHOLAS CABASILAS

THE LIFE IN CHRIST

Translated from the Greek
by
CARMINO J. deCATANZARO

With an Introduction
by
BORIS BOBRINSKOY
Professor of Dogmatic Theology
St. Sergius Orthodox Theological Institute
Paris, France

ST. VLADIMIR'S SEMINARY PRESS
1974

ISBN 0-913836-12-5

PRINTED IN THE UNITED STATES OF AMERICA

Table of Contents

THE THIRD BOOK

THE FOURTH BOOK

THE FIFTH BOOK

THE SIXTH BOOK

THE SEVENTH BOOK

Translator's Foreword

1. The Author and his Time

Political decay, yet astounding richness in the things of the spirit—such is the picture presented by the Byzantine world of the fourteenth century. Faced with increasing aggression on the part of the Ottoman Turks, the once proud Eastern Roman empire maintained a precarious hold on its shrinking territories. Its outward dominion steadily diminished, yet its intellectual and artistic vigour actually increased right up to that fateful day of May 28, 1453, when Mohammed the Conqueror broke through the walls of Constantinople and the emperor Constantine XI died in the defence of his city.

It was the century which produced the mosaics of the Church of the Twelve Apostles in Thessalonica and those of the Church of the Chora (Kariye Cami) in Constantinople, as well as many of the frescoes of the churches in the ruined city of Mystras in the Peloponnesus. It was also a century of great theological activity and even bitter controversy. In this area Nicholas Cabasilas was a prominent figure.

Much obscurity has surrounded his life and career because of confusion with his maternal uncle, Nilus Cabasilas, who followed Saint Gregory Palamas in the see of Thessalonica in 1351. In part this is due to Nicholas having adopted his uncle's surname instead of that of his father,

Chamaetos. Only recently has this confusion been completely unravelled, largely through the efforts of the Greek scholar Athanasios A. Angelopoulos, on whose work, *Nikolaos Kavasilas Hamaetos—His Life and His Work,* published in Greek by the Vlatadon Monastery in Thessalonica in 1970, we have drawn for the following data.

Nicholas Cabasilas was born in Thessalonica in 1322 or 1323. He received an excellent education, first in his home city and then in Constantinople. There he entered the imperial service, and for a decade was prominent as an official and friend of the emperor John VI Cantacuzenos, who entrusted him with various important missions, including a very difficult one to his home city, which was torn by social upheaval and party strife. When John VI was deposed in 1354 and retired to monastic life, Nicholas retired from political life and devoted himself to philosophy and theology.

It is in this latter period that we find him entering upon an ecclesiastical career. It used to be thought that Nicholas, like his uncle Nilus Cabasilas, became bishop of his native city. This has now been shown to be unlikely. The records of the see know nothing of him in that capacity. Nor on the other hand, as has been more recently maintained, did he remain a layman. It has now been established that he entered the Manganon monastery near Constantinople, and that he probably became a priest.

This was also the period of his greatest literary activity. Nothing is certain about the date of his death, though he appears to have continued his activity past the tragic fall of his native Thessalonica to the Turks in 1387.

2. Literary and Theological Work

The literary legacy of Nicholas Cabasilas is abundant and varied, reflecting his activities both as a civil administrator and a churchman. In the former sphere we find him keenly concerned with social justice, a problem which was becoming acute in the decaying state of the empire.

His aristocratic background and support of the Cantacuzeni did not blind him to the social abuses which had caused the risings of the "Zealots" in his native city. In the latter sphere we find reflected the ecclesiastical controversies of the day.

One of these was the very practical problem of relations with the Latin West. Reconciliation with the papacy and alliance with the Latin powers were politically desirable because of the Turkish menace, and various attempts were made which culminated in the ill-fated Council of Florence in the following century (1438-1445). Latinizers were active in the Byzantine empire in Cabasilas' day, including his friend Demetrios Kydones. The claim has been made that he was of their party. It is clear that he was well acquainted with Latin theology, as is evident from the echoes of St. Anselm that we find in *The Life in Christ* (e.g., p. 118); it is equally clear from his *Commentary on the Divine Liturgy* that he could be quite critical of Latin theology where it conflicted with Orthodoxy, although, very interestingly, he takes a kindly view of the Roman Canon of the Mass and equates its prayer *Supplices te rogamus* with the Epiclesis in the Byzantine rite.

The other great controversy of the day was that surrounding hesychast spirituality. This was no question of theological technicalities, but rather of a theology of Christian experience on its highest level, that of mysticism. How could one maintain the reality of *theosis,* "deification" of man, without breaking the distinction between Creator and creature? Could there be a real vision of God on the part of mystics which was not a vision of His essence? Saint Gregory Palamas, the great protagonist of hesychasm, was bishop of Cabasilas' native city from 1350-59, and Cabasilas wrote a treatise against St. Gregory's opponent, Nicephoros Gregoras. There is therefore no basis whatsoever for the attempt which has been made to claim Cabasilas as an opponent of Palamism. It is true that in *The Life in Christ* he makes no direct reference to the typical Palamite distinction between the essence and the "energies" of God, but then neither does Saint Gregory himself in his homilies to his flock at Thessalonica. Both are addressing themselves neither to monks nor solitaries, nor even to professional theologians, but to those who are seeking to live the life in Christ in the world. On the other hand, there is nothing in *The Life in Christ* which is not entirely compatible with Palamism; in fact, as Lot-Borodine and Bobrinskoy have pointed out, the work abounds with clear hints of it.

It is Christian experience which is at the centre of our author's concern in *The Life in Christ,* a Christian experience in which the sacramental life is crucial, but a sacramental life which is rich in prayer and meditation, as is abundantly apparent in books VI and VII. Here we may notice several features which may strike the Western reader as strange. The author in his book deals with only three Mysteries, to use the Eastern term which has been retained throughout the translation—Baptism, Chrismation (corresponding to Western "Confirmation"), and the Eucharist—and includes a rite which is not a Mystery as such, that of the consecration of a church. While the Latin Church had accepted the number of seven Sacraments ever since the time of Peter Lombard (c. 1150), the situation in the Orthodox East was much more fluid at this time. Though the sevenfold enumeration has since become conventional among the Orthodox as well, one is left with a distinct impression that Orthodoxy is less inclined than either the Latin Church or Protestantism to classify the operations of the grace of God in either this or any other area.

Again to the Western reader, whose background is that of centuries of discussion on the problem of the relation of the sacramental sign to the divine gift in the Sacrament, the sacramental realism of our author may come as something of a shock. Protestants in particular, and not a few Anglicans, will find statements about the baptismal water producing spiritual effects suggestive of a mechanistic, if not magical, approach to the Sacraments. This is hardly fair to the author, or to Orthodox in general. Here is no blindness to the fact that many who are baptized or receive any other Sacrament do not show corresponding fruits in their lives.

Rather, he constantly stresses the need for man's co-operation with the gifts of God.

Some Western Christians might take exception to the author's stress on man's contribution toward his own salvation. Here it must be openly admitted that Eastern Orthodoxy has escaped the domination of St. Augustine's thought which is so marked a feature of Western Christianity, Catholic or Protestant, whether in terms of exaggeration of that great Father, as in Jansenism and Calvinism, or of reaction against him. Orthodoxy is not, and cannot be Pelagian. Apart from the action of God in Jesus Christ and the Holy Spirit man cannot be saved. There is no question of man being able to save himself merely by responding to revealed truth. But equally emphatically Orthodoxy cannot regard man as an automaton. Here again Cabasilas is very careful to emphasize that man has a real, though limited part in his own salvation. Orthodoxy has never been bedevilled with a theology of "merit," as has been the case with Latin theology, to which Protestants and Anglicans rightly reacted by its total rejection.

3. The Translation

The present version is the first in English of *The Life in Christ*. Besides earlier Latin and French versions, it has been translated into Russian (Moscow, 1874), French (by S. Broussaleux, Amay, 1932, reprinted in 1962), and German (by G. Hoch, introduction by Endre von Ivánka, Munich, 1957). In addition to these the "Zoe" Brotherhood of Theologians has published an abridgement and paraphrase in modern Greek (Athens, 1964). Of his other major writings the only one to appear in English translation has been his *Commentary on the Divine Liturgy,* translated by J. M. Hussey and P. A. McNulty and published by S. P. C. K. in 1960.

The present version has been made from the Greek text contained in Migne's *Patrologia Graeca,* vol. 150, originally edited by W. Gall of Greifswald in 1849. For a small section, 553 bcd, 557d - 560 ab, use has been made of the text on pages 114-115 of the monograph of Athanasios A. Angelopoulos. To facilitate reference to the original the numbers of the columns of the Migne text have been indicated at the top of alternate pages.

Biblical references generally follow the Revised Standard Version except for the Psalter, where the Prayer Book version has been used as being closer to the Septuagint text used by Cabasilas. Where necessary the translation has been adjusted to conform to the Septuagint. In such cases the abbreviation "LXX" has been added to the biblical reference. Where the text is merely alluded to, or quoted loosely, this has been indicated by prefixing "cf."

The French and German versions, as well as the modern Greek, have been frequently consulted, with the German version in particular as suggesting improvements in Gall's Greek text.

The division into sections, as well as the headings, while often suggested by the modern Greek and French versions, are mainly the translator's own. Headings of sections, as well as a few explanatory phrases and words not occurring in the original, have been enclosed in square brackets. The paragraphs within brackets on pages 157 and 158 have been supplied from the text referred to in the monograph of Angelopoulos.

*   *   *

The translator expresses his gratitude to Orthodox and Anglican friends for their encouragement to persevere in this project. In particular he would single out the Very Reverend Dr. John Meyendorff of St. Vladimir's Orthodox Theological Seminary, New York, Mrs. Margaret Lisney of Witchford Vicarage, near Ely, England, the Very Reverend Archimandrite Eusebius A. Stephanou of Fort Wayne, Indiana, and the Community of the Sisters of the Church, Oakville, Ontario.

In thankfulness to Almighty God he presents this work, conscious of its imperfections and of the debt which he owes to his predecessors, as an offering of love and veneration to that great Church which, more than any other, has preserved intact the rich heritage of patristic faith and spirituality, a heritage which in our own times has proved its vitality in the lives and witness of confessors without number as well as numerous martyrs. With it he offers the prayer that God may use this version to inspire Christian men and women, both within and without the visible body of Orthodoxy, to live that "life which is hid with Christ in God."

C. J. DE C.
St. Barnabas', Ottawa

Introduction

NICHOLAS CABASILAS:
THEOLOGY AND SPIRITUALITY*

BORIS BOBRINSKOY

Nicholas Cabasilas' two works of sacramental and liturgical theology probably belong to the last period of his
life, when the ardour of his political and religious passions
was subdued, and when far from the public arena, he could
consecrate himself to a written exposition of his spiritual
vision. We have in him a remarkable combination of the
humanist, philosopher and savant—a statesman not only in
civil affairs but equally in those of the Church; an orator,
a theologian, a mystic: "neither monk, nor priest nor hermit
fleeing from the world to study in solitude, who yet pro-
foundly influenced his contemporaries by his moral and
intellectual qualities as much as by the superiority of his
principles yet without withdrawing from the society of his
equals or indeed from the common feelings of humanity."[1]

*A reprint of the second and main part of Fr. Bobrinskoy's study on
Cabasilas, which appeared in *Sobornost*, series 5: No. 7 (Autumn, 1968),
pp. 483-505. We refer the reader to that edition for a complete bibliography
on Cabasilas and for more historical information on his career. We thank
the Editor of *Sobornost* for the kind permission to reprint the study.

1. Nicholas and Hesychasm

After a first and somewhat superficial reading of the
writings of Cabasilas one may get the impression that the
hesychast disputes left little mark either on his thought or
his terminology. This is, for example, the opinion of Endre
von Ivanka[2] and of B. Tatakis. The latter recognises Nicholas
Cabasilas as "a fervent palamite and as the pre-eminent
mystical theologian of his time," but affirms nevertheless,
"that there are few evidences of palamism in his mysticism."[3]
At the end of the hesychast controversy, about 1354, he
did certainly write a short pamphlet "against the arguments
of Gregoras,"[4] in which he states his admiration for Gregory
Palamas, "one of the greatest and most holy among the
Thessalonians." But in his pre-eminently spiritual writings
he makes no mention either of the events or of the problems
and terminology of palamism, and in particular he says
nothing of the distinction between the divine essence and the
uncreated energies—nor of the doctrine of the light of
Tabor in the Transfiguration: nor yet of the psychophysical
method of pure prayer which was denigrated by the op-
ponents of Palamas by the name of "omphaloscopy."

Is it in reality possible to speak of Cabasilas' insensitivity
in relation to hesychasm? Does the supposed opposition between the social humanism and the sacramental spirituality
of a Cabasilas and the hesychast mysticism of the Athonite
solitaries, hostile to all secular knowledge, belong to the
objective reality of Byzantine religion? We do not think so.
If, as John Meyendorff says, on the one hand, "as in all
movements of a popular nature, Byzantine hesychasm did
not always escape a certain obscurantism," and on the other,
"the humanists started from the assumption of a sort of
autonomy for human reason, and its independence in relation
to God whom they conceived as impenetrable and inacces-
sible,"[5] Cabasilas gives us the example of a humanist in
the true sense of the word, who honoured all the resources
of the human mind and heart, but who nevertheless brought
all these values into unreserved subjection to the Kingdom
and love of Christ. "By his nature, his will and his mind,"

writes Cabasilas, "man is drawn to Christ. . . . Christ is the centre of all human aspirations and becomes the delight of the mind. That any thought or loving aspiration be set on aught but him is to turn from the one thing necessary, is to betray the original likeness impressed on our nature."[6]

We shall see how close the Christocentric sacramentalism of Nicholas Cabasilas is to the heart of the spiritual message of palamite hesychasm.

The manifold spiritual wealth of Orthodoxy cannot be contained in one particular system or one single theological language. The mystical temperament of a St. Gregory of Nyssa or of the author of the Areopagitica in no way excludes a theology which is sacramental and pastoral such as is found, for example, in St. Irenaeus, St. John Chrysostom and St. Cyril of Jerusalem, whose aim was to teach their flocks the fundamentals of the faith and Christian living. There is a close and organic union between the different forms of theological language and the different degrees and directions of the Christian faith. The mysticism of hesychasm, the interior recollection and the drawing of the mind into the heart, presupposes a particular kind of vocation, intelligible to those who have been called to follow it, a life of asceticism, renunciation of the world and discipline of the will in monastic solitude, and in the spirit of obedience. On the contrary the sacramental vision, the participation in the universal mysteries of the Church, is the royal way open to all and obligatory not only for ascetics but for all Christian people. Hesychasm is not an end in itself but a special way of perfection, and by this very fact plays an important part in the unity of the Body. On the one hand it is a particular way of sanctification, and on the other a showing forth to the whole Church of a fundamental element of prophetic freedom and liberty of spirit in the search for the one thing necessary. The dimension of hesychasm with its experience of the vision of the light of Tabor and of pure prayer must be integrated into the spiritual and catholic tradition of Orthodoxy. If it remains apart from this it becomes sterile and bears no fruit.

It would therefore be inexact to limit the living and

creative theology of the 14th century to the dogmatic statements of the palamite doctrine of the essence and the
energies. Rather it is essential to understand the traditional
and existential truth of this doctrine in the growth of the
knowledge of the living God. The theological activity of
St. Gregory Palamas, the chief doctor and defender of the
principles of the Athonite tradition "of the holy hesychasts,"
is justified mainly by the fulness of his spirituality and
asceticism and his profound knowledge of the Fathers.

But it would be a mistake to see in palamism nothing
except the affirmation of the doctrine most contested by
its adversaries. The principal aim of Palamas' pastoral activity
was to preserve without confusion but also without division
the two "poles" of the Christian theology of salvation:
(a) the absolute transcendence of the being and life of
God and the incomprehensibility of his essence, (b) the
true and not merely metaphorical possibility for the Christian
to participate in the fulness of the divine life and the gifts
of the Holy Spirit in their greatest intensity, culminating in
the transfiguration and deification of the whole man (spirit,
soul, mind, body) by the uncreated energies of the Trinity.
The essential teaching of St. Gregory Palamas in his pastoral
and ascetical works *(Homilies, Treatise on the Defence of
the Holy Hesychasts, Chapters Physical and Theological,
Letters, Chapters on Prayer and Purity of Heart)* not less
than in his more controversial writings is that by the Incarnation and Redemption of the Incarnate Word on the one
hand, and by the participation of man in the Holy Mysteries
of the Church, by prayer and ascetic discipline on the other,
the deification of human nature is realizable in this earthly
life—here and now.

Palamas was not only an austere monk, a hesychast
enduring all the rigour of solitude on the Holy Mountain or
an indefatigable controversialist hardened to the arguments
and intricacies of dialectic. In the last phase of his life after
the triumph of Orthodoxy and his accession to the archi-
episcopal throne of Thessalonika, the pastoral qualities of St.
Gregory Palamas were revealed in all their fulness: he gave
himself to preaching and teaching the fundamentals of faith

and piety.[7] With the exception of the two homilies on the Transfiguration[8] he makes no mention in his sermons of the controversy concerning the divine energies. He transmits to his hearers in his almost daily preaching the essentials of the Christian faith—the unfathomable Mystery of the Incarnation and Redemption, the reality of the Christian's participation in salvation and in the divine grace by the sacramental life of the Church, and his acceptance of all the means that contribute to his sanctification.

"It is not therefore," writes J. Meyendorff, "from outside the Church that the hesychasts drew their mysticism of the Name of Jesus and their anthropology, but from the whole tradition of the Church. Nothing shows better than the homilies of Palamas to what degree that handful of subtle intellectuals who continued after 1351 to oppose palamism had failed to grasp, in the manner Gregory himself had done, the everyday realities and deep feelings of popular piety of the Byzantine Church."[9]

2. Nicholas Cabasilas' Sacramental Mysticism

The method of prayer of Athonite hesychasm and its specifically monastic slant are not to be found in the homilies of St. Gregory Palamas nor do they enter directly into the sacramental perspective of Nicholas Cabasilas. It is clear that this silence of Cabasilas about the doctrine of hesychasm is in no way due either to indifference or to hostility to this teaching. This is moreover the opinion of M. Lot-Borodine, one of the most penetrating authorities on the spirituality of Cabasilas, who writes, "The author [i.e., Nicholas] although fully in agreement with Gregory Palamas, having himself assuredly practised the hesychast method, did not wish in a work destined to be read by the faithful to make open propaganda in favour of what was not really an essential part of his cataphatic teaching; a teaching mainly directed towards the mysticism of a Love wholly sacrificial and so aflame with the divine joy of being totally possessed by him and possessing him."[10]

Cabasilas was not by temperament a solitary. He did not experience the need to withdraw himself for communion with his God. The "law of Love" is the basis of his spirituality as he writes in the sixth book of *The Life in Christ*. "This law demands no arduous nor afflicting work, nor loss of money; it does not involve shame, nor any dishonour, nor anything worse; it puts no obstacle in the pursuit of any art or profession. The general keeps the power to command, the labourer can work the ground, the artisan can carry on with his occupation. There is no reason to retire into solitude, to eat unusual food, to be inadequately clothed, or endanger one's health, or to resort to any other special endeavour; it suffices to give oneself wholly to meditation and to remain always within oneself without depriving the world of one's talents."[11]

Cabasilas is not here belittling monasticism or ascetic endeavour. But the very labours of ascetics cannot be sustained without continual recourse to divine grace, the Eucharistic food and intimacy with Christ. "So weak is our nature," says Cabasilas, "that the wisest among men, even after baptismal regeneration, and after partaking of the heavenly banquet of the altar, that hearth of living flames, have so little steadfastness or virtue that they know the necessity for frequent communion, for the purifying blood and for the grace which comes from on high, if they do not wish to fall into great spiritual indigence. Witness those ascetics who have taken on themselves great labours from a good and virtuous motive and who afterwards gave themselves up to the worst excesses; the anchorites who set out for the hills, fleeing from all noise, all society, as they would from the plague, to immerse themselves in God, who practised virtues in the highest perfection of which a man is capable, who did great things for God, and yet because they did not put their whole confidence and hope in God alone, suddenly gave themselves up to the worst kind of licentiousness and for whom no infamy was too bad."[12]

The Life in Christ of Nicholas Cabasilas introduces us to a life filled with the intimacy of God's all-pervading presence which is nearer to those who invoke him than their own heart, and which comes to us even if we be sinful, for he is good. "At every hour invoke him, he who is the object of our meditations, in order that our spirit may be always absorbed in him and our attention each day centred on him. To call on him there is no need for any lengthy preparation in prayer, nor for some special place, nor for reiterated groans. In effect he is nowhere absent; it is impossible that he should not be in us, for to all those who seek him he is closer than our own heart."[13]

It is precisely this "Life in Christ" which is the existential centre of attraction common to hesychasm and to the spirituality of Cabasilas. Union with Christ, according to Cabasilas, must be understood in the most literal and realistic manner. He would invite us through the sacraments to a true "Christification." This line of thought belonged to the patristic tradition,[14] and in particular to Gregory Palamas.[15] The Eucharistic communion is not only a powerful means of sanctification but is the supreme end, and the very essence of our life in Christ. By frequent communion a deep and radical change takes place within us, "the Blood of Christ transforms the human heart into a sanctuary for God more beautiful than the temple of Solomon."[16]

"O wonder of wonders," cries Cabasilas, "that Christ's spirit is united to our spirit, his will is one with ours, his flesh becomes our flesh, his blood flows in our veins. What spirit is ours when it is possessed by his, our will when led captive by his, our clay when set on fire by his flame!"[17] Cabasilas' debt to biblical and Pauline sources is apparent in all the development of his thought. He frequently refers to St. Paul in order to find confirmation for his own experience of intimacy with Christ, by whom he is possessed and indwelt. "It is God himself we touch [in the Eucharist]," says Cabasilas, "and God becomes one with us in the closest union. What could be more intimate than to be one spirit with God?"[18]

By this invasion of Christ into our inmost self the transformation is complete and human nature by the power of God is truly supernaturalized. "An energizing power coming into contact with an inferior one does not leave it as it was;

the iron in the fire is no longer iron. . . . So it is evident that
when Christ enters into us and becomes one with us we are
transfigured, we are immersed in him as a single drop of
water is lost in a vast ocean of perfume."[19]

The doctrine of palamism is centred on the mystery of the
Incarnation and the life of Christ in the soul of the Christian, through the practice of prayer, asceticism and the sacraments of the Church. "Christ has become our brother," says
Palamas, "by becoming like unto us in flesh and blood. He
has bound us closely to himself as a husband is bound to
his wife; so that he by communicating to us his blood makes
us one with himself. He has also become our Father in
baptism, which makes us like unto him, and he feeds us
at his own breast as a tender mother nourishes her own
children. Come, said Christ, eat of my flesh and drink of
my blood . . . not only that you may be made after God's
image, but that you may become kings and gods, eternal
and heavenly, by putting on me, thy King and God."[20]

Almost identical images are to be found in Cabasilas.
There is a common inspiration. "He is our Host and our
dwelling place"[21] . . . "God comes to earth and in so doing
ennobles man. He becomes man and he deifies man. . . . For
as it was impossible for us to rise up to him and to share
in his heavenly treasures, so he comes down to us to share
our life. . . . He gives himself to us, for by communicating
of his body and blood we receive God into ourselves. . . ."[22]
"The Saviour, in order to be our Father and to be able to
say, "Here am I, I and the children that God has given me"
(Is. 8:18), has assumed our flesh and blood. So likewise to
become his children, we must share his very life and thus
through this sacrament we become not only his members
but his children. . . ."[23] "There remains truly but one birth
and sonship, that which unites us to Christ, and in this is
absorbed our natural sonship."[24]

By frequent communion, so necessary for human frailty,
"a veritable transference of deifying energy operates in us."[25]
"He is the Host who fills the dwelling with his presence, for
it is his very self that we possess, not a part; we do not
receive some rays but the Sun of Righteousness himself, so

that we are penetrated by him and become one spirit with him; body and soul and all the faculties are deified when there is union of soul with Soul, body with Body, blood with Blood."[26]

It is in this context of life in Christ understood as an interpenetration and radical transformation of flesh by Flesh, blood by Blood, as an organic union of the divine and human natures in the transfigured body of the Christian that is found Cabasilas' doctrine of the Sacred Heart of Christ. This is where he departs from hesychasm and shows his originality and the boldness and vigour of his personal inspiration. The importance of the heart in the spiritual life is central in traditional orthodox spirituality. In contrast with the intellectual mysticism inspired by neoplatonism and represented in Eastern Christianity by Origen, Evagrius and their disciples, it is the heart, and not the mind freed from the embarrassments of the body, which in biblical theology and in authentic orthodox spirituality is pre-eminently the prime mover, not only of our physiological and affective life but also of the life of the spirit.

For both in the Evangelists and in all the Scriptures we find it is in the heart that the most intimate and secret decisions arise. "For out of the abundance of the heart the mouth speaks" (Matt. 12:34). "For what comes out of the mouth proceeds from the heart, . . . all evil thoughts and impurities" (Matt. 15:18-19). Orthodox spiritual tradition, overcoming a real temptation in its history to embrace a spirituality platonic in origin, returned to that sense of the heart as the only centre of our being, and through it to that sense of the whole man and the whole creation which was assumed by the second Person of the Trinity at the Incarnation. For the Pseudo-Macarius, the author of the Spiritual Homilies, the power of the Holy Spirit is manifested in the heart. "The heart is in effect the Master and King of the whole body and when grace has permeated the inmost recesses of the heart, it controls all our actions and our thoughts, for there the mind, and all the thoughts of the soul are to be found, and thence comes all good. So that thus grace penetrates into all the members of the body."[27] According to one of the greatest masters of primitive hesychasm, St. John Climacus (580-650), the very essence of monasticism is the search for God within oneself. "The hesychast is the one who says, 'My heart is steadfast O God, my heart is steadfast' (Ps. 57:8). The hesychast is one who says, 'I sleep but my heart waketh' (Cant. 5:2). Close the door of your cell to all fleshly desires; the door of your lips to the words you would speak; the door of your spirit to all other spirits."[28]

St. Gregory Palamas sought to show how in reality there was only verbal opposition between the intellectualism of a St. Gregory of Nyssa and the biblical point of view of the Pseudo-Macarius.[29] For Palamas, Christ taking to himself a human body and penetrating it with his divinity, "makes of us a temple of his divinity and enlightens our soul from within."[30]

The true originality of Nicholas Cabasilas was to introduce the traditional theme of the heart into his exposition of sacramental spirituality in that Christocentric perspective which was so dear to him. The first mention that Cabasilas makes of the image of the heart is in connection with the theme of frequent communion. "It is surely through this blessed Heart that the virtue which flows from the holy table brings forth in us the true life.... The Bread of Life much more than any other rite transforms us into the body of Christ. For as it is by the head and the heart that the members live, 'so he that eats of me even he shall live by me' (Jn. 6:58).... In conformity with what is the usual role of the head and heart we are changed and live, even as Christ himself lives.... As he is Life, he breathes it into us through his own Spirit. He communicates life to us even as the heart and the head to the members of the body...."[31] The physiological realism of Cabasilas is astonishing when he seeks to describe the degree of intimacy of our union with Christ in Eucharistic communion.

By the invitation "Receive" (Matt. 26:26), "it is clear we are invited to a feast, at which we truly receive Christ in our hands, we take him into our mouths, his soul is made one with our soul, his Body with our body, his Blood flows in our veins."[32] So "the sacred meal effects between Christ and us a closer union than that which was realized by our parents when they begat us. In truth he does not only share with us some particles of his flesh or some drops of his blood, but gives us both in all their fullness: he is not only a principle of life as are our parents, but in very truth Life itself."[33]

It is from the heart of Jesus and not from any natural cause that this vital principle of life is infused into the veins and blood of the communicants. "It is his own blood that he pours into the heart of communicants, so that his own life may be born in us."[34] By this vivifying transfusion the royalty of Christ becomes effective over the life of men. "This is how he exercised his royalty in purity and truth over men . . . for he is more gracious to us than a friend, more impartial than a sovereign, more gentle than a father, closer to us than our own self, more vital to us than our own heart."[35] Thus by the life-giving presence of Christ, the body becomes the temple of his living Spirit. And Cabasilas grows even more bold: the members of Christ "will never taste death" (Jn. 8:52)—"in effect how can these members die who depend for life on a heart that is always alive?"[36]

This same doctrine of the living Head[37] and life-giving Heart from which flow the sanctification of the members of the body is also to be found faithfully portrayed in the *Commentary on the Divine Liturgy*, in those chapters dedicated to the theology of communion. Explaining those words of the priest at the elevation of the Bread of Life, "Holy things to the holy," Cabasilas writes, "The faithful are called saints because of the holy thing of which they partake, because of him whose body and blood they receive. Members of his body, flesh of his flesh, and bone of his bone, as long as we remain united to him and preserve our connection with him, we live by holiness, drawing into ourselves through the holy mysteries the sanctity which comes from that Head and that Heart. But if we should cut ourselves off, if we should separate ourselves from the unity of this most holy Body, we partake of the holy mysteries in vain, for life cannot flow into dead and amputated limbs."[38]

Commenting, a few lines further on, on the symbolism

of the Zeon, he declares, "The Church is represented in the
holy mysteries, not in figure only, but as the limbs are
represented in the heart . . . for here is no mere sharing of
a name, or analogy by resemblance, but an identity of
actuality. . . ."[39] If one could see the Church of Christ, insofar
as she is united to him and shares in his sacred Body, one
would see nothing other than the Body of the Lord. . . ."[40]
Henceforth the faithful, through the Blood of Christ, live
in Christ truly dependent on that divine Head and clothed
with that all-holy Body."[41]

We agree wholeheartedly with Myrrha Lot-Borodine,[42]
that this theme of the heart of Christ, this heart triumphant
and overflowing with blessedness, is in reality the key which
opens the door to the whole of Cabasilas' synthesis. In agreement with (and not in opposition to) the image of Christ
as Head of his Body the Church, Cabasilas shows with great
depth the overflowing love and compassion of Christ in the
life of the believer, this communication of life and intimacy
which is of the very essence of the Eucharistic mystery. His
showing of the heart of Christ in a perspective both ecclesial
and Eucharistic is certainly in contrast with that of the indi-
vidual and pietistic devotion to the Sacred Heart of Jesus
in the West.[43] The realistic anthropology of this Byzantine
theologian, and anterior to him of the whole hesychast tradition, shows us the way in which this unique symbol of love
and intimacy could be used as a means of "union" between
the East and the West.[44]

The "objective" realism of Cabasilas never leads him to
neglect the more "subjective" side of the Eucharistic life. Far
from it, the second part of *The Life in Christ* concentrates on
teaching the infinite compassion and love of God and man's
response to it. By the meditation on and memory of this love,
by a wonder and gratitude continually renewed, the Christian,
after the example of Christ, becomes the man living in the
spirit of the Beatitudes.

No less than by his Christocentric sacramental doctrine,
Nicholas Cabasilas is close to the hesychastic tradition by
all his teaching on ceaseless vigilance, awareness, and contemplation of the love of God. If he shows great discretion

in all that pertains to ascetic exercises and mortification, if he warns us against the excesses of contrition ("fear, shame, contrition, mortification are alone worthwhile when they have God as their end"),[45] nevertheless he does encourage the Christian to a faithful constancy in humility and purity, in forgiveness and kindness, and in a joyful co-operation of the free will with the grace of God.

The ascetic doctrine of hesychasm concerning the invisible warfare, the guard of the heart and ceaseless prayer, is praised and given particular stress by Cabasilas. But above all it is in the Eucharistic life that the heart of the spiritual conflict is seen in all its fulness. The "holy table shows us how to make a real use of the strength (baptismal) and armour (chrismatic unction) granted to us, to seek perfection not by letting ourselves be carried or pushed along, but rather as athletes spontaneously going forth to take their part in a race."[46] Further on, Cabasilas, speaking of that night when no man can work, goes on to say, "As soon as the sun is risen, and its rays are dispersed far and wide by the sacraments, it behoves us to begin this arduous work of labour without delay; and with the sweat of our brow, to win this Bread broken for us, and according to the invitation of our Lord to work for 'the food which endures to eternal life' (Jn. 7:27): words in which are enshrined the order to approach the holy table, not as idle and inactive men but as the bond slaves of the Lord."[47]

If Cabasilas enjoins Christians to fight and take their part in Christ's battle, his pastoral compassion seeks to prevent despair in this arduous struggle. "It is Christ himself," he says, "who invites us to this sacred banquet, who is our companion in this fight. . . . By the Eucharist he dwells within us and helps us to gain the prize. . . . When there is need for courage and constancy to gain the victory, Jesus Christ takes it upon himself to provide us with all that we need through the grace of baptism and chrismation. When he fights beside us he expects us to do our best, and when there is any question of reward he hides himself completely."[48]

Nothing can encourage us more in the fight and stimulate the ardour of the victor than the remembrance of God: to recall with gratitude his free and 'mad love' for man the perverse sinner. "That which inspires us in the conflict is the ardent desire to gain the prize: this desire will make every struggle however arduous seem light. And nothing so enflames the desire for what is perfect than to keep the thought of it uppermost in our minds and to realize how desirable it is. It was this fire which burnt in the heart of the prophet when he contemplated his God. 'My heart was hot within me, and while I was thus musing the fire kindled' " (Ps. 39:4 PBV).[49]

The burning love for God—this is the means by which he draws us to himself, this is the fire which enflames our will and awakens in us the desire for the spiritual conflict. This love of God does not constrain nor force the free will of man. On the contrary it is patient, humble, and awaits our response: "God is not content to remain where he is and call unto him the bond-slave he loves so dearly, but he descends and seeks for him himself. He, the Almighty, stoops to the lowliness of our poverty. He comes himself, declares his love for us, and it seems almost that he is asking a favour of us. When we refuse he does not withdraw, he is not wounded by our rejection; rebuffed, he waits at the door, does all to show his abiding love; he takes on himself all these humiliations and dies."[50]

Such is the meaning of the precepts of Christ and how he conformed his life to the divine precepts. These are "therefore not beyond the power of human fulfilment . . . every Christian is perfectly aware that he is obliged to put them into practice . . . they are obligatory for all the faithful . . . and possible for all who have a good will."[51]

"That is why," Cabasilas concludes, in extolling the Eucharistic life, "whoever has resolved to live the Christ-life, must, for there is no other source of life, live in union with his mind and heart, which is impossible unless there is identity of purpose." "It is therefore true that it is impossible to live in independence of this life-giving heart and we destroy in fact this life line when we do not will what he wills."[52]

In Cabasilas' teaching in *The Life in Christ* which relates to the subjective aspect of prayer, it is possible to distinguish, in agreement with Myrrha Lot-Borodine,[53] two ways of growth in knowledge of and familiarity with God: these are meditation and prayer in its more exact sense. She says in her book on Nicholas Cabasilas entitled *A Master of Byzantine Spirituality of the Fourteenth Century:* "The Byzantine Master urges us with an authority and verve, rare, if not unique in the Christian East, to use our *imagination* to reconstruct and to see as though we had been present the living and inspiring realities which are incarnate in the Person of the Saviour. . . . The author is himself one who visualises, and he insists unhesitatingly that we must see in order to experience, and assimilate *with all our powers* the wonder of the One and only Beautiful. In this sense it is possible to affirm that for Cabasilas meditation has the nature of an experience and that an important one."[54]

Meditation which is directed, inspired, and willed by the desire, the passion, and the love for Christ, is not passive prayer or pure contemplation. On the contrary it must be an exercise which is continuous and constant, sustained by a spiritual endeavour which is ever moving towards the divine Ideal, and so a true beginning in the following of the footsteps of Christ. This idea is to grow upon us with an increasing power born from the seeking of the "one thing necessary."[55] All the hesychast experience of vigilance and the mindfulness of God is here applied by Cabasilas to meditation on the infinite love of God for us.

But meditation which centres on the discipline of the will and imagination, transformed and inspired by the love of Christ, is not for Cabasilas the end of our spiritual endeavour. This is to be found rather in "mental prayer" properly so called, unceasing prayer, of which Cabasilas speaks with great discretion, but which he must surely have known and practised in conformity with the ideas both of traditional and contemporary hesychasm.

The aim of pure prayer or prayer of the heart is to fulfil the gospel command "to pray without ceasing": this prayer blends the invocation of the holy Name with the prayer of the publican, "Lord be merciful to me a sinner." By unceasing repetition of the Name of Jesus the believer seeks to enter a deeper and more complete union with God, regulating his breathing and his pulse in unison with the repetition of the holy Name. "May the memory of Jesus become one with each breath you breathe," teaches St. John Climacus in his *Ladder of Perfection*. This presence of Christ realized by the invocation of his holy Name has nothing mechanical about it, but is the answer of Christ to the call of the heart which seeks and thirsts for the presence of God.

The content of the prayer of Jesus is therefore the divine Name of Jesus Christ. In the Bible there is a close affinity between the name and the person. To call on the Name of God is to know that he is within us. For St. Paul the Name of Jesus is inexpressible and above every name (Phil. 2:9-11); and Hermas says, "the Name of the Son of God sustains the whole world."[56]

There is a passage in *The Life in Christ* which explicitly directs the believer to this type of prayer. "We invoke the Name of God with our lips and also in our desires and thoughts in order that in everything we have done amiss we may apply the only health-giving remedy: for there is no other Name under heaven whereby we may be saved" (Acts 4:12).[57]

Cabasilas proposes none of the usual techniques which would necessitate either a particular preparation or initiation, or some special place suitable for silence and solitude. "To call on the Name," he says, "no unusual preparation for prayer is needed, no special place nor much speaking.... For truly, he is always present; we can be nowhere without him even for a single moment and to those who seek, he is closer to them than the beat of their heart."[58]

If therefore the practice of the Jesus prayer is from the point of view of Orthodox tradition considered to be the art of arts, and if those who have mastered it are considered to have reached the heights of perfection and sanctity, nevertheless each Christian can draw great profit from the practice, discovering from it the secrets of the interior life. By it we create the right spiritual atmosphere for the development of the liturgical life, and so give to that life the necessary quality and inspiration which belong to this living dialogue, and pass beyond the stage which mainly considers the multiplicity of words. This is why the prayer of the heart presupposes great self-discipline and a continual spiritual awareness. If only a small number can attain to the higher degrees of the perfection of the prayer of the heart, its first fruits are accessible to all, and are the condition for a real transformation of our human nature by the Holy Spirit. So Cabasilas will add with a scarcely veiled allusion to the Jesus prayer: "In fact nothing is impossible for those who invoke the holy Name, not by reason of their virtues, but in order to glorify him whose Name they invoke."[59]

This then is the position that the way of pure prayer holds in Cabasilas' synthesis. We need not be surprised about his silence regarding the hesychast "methods." The context of his spirituality is different. "Palamas himself," says J. Meyendorff in his introduction to the study of Gregory Palamas, "was certainly not antagonistic to this technique, but found it unnecessary to keep on referring to this secondary and very localized aspect of the hesychasm of his time."[60]

At the heart of his teaching on mental prayer Cabasilas would unite that interior Eucharist which is the uninterrupted invocation of the Name, with the frequent partaking of the heavenly Bread which is the sacramental root of the presence of Christ in the believer's heart. "The Bread which is in truth the very source of life to the heart of man will produce this fruit in our lives [i.e., the incessant invocation], will give us the energy for our contemplation, will cast out from our soul all indifference which takes root within; for this Bread comes from heaven to bring us life and it is this Bread which we must seek by every means to feed on. We must in order not to grow hungry feed at this Eucharistic banquet continually."[61] "The real presence" of Christ both by the invocation of the Name and by communion of his Eucharistic body, this is the way and end of the life which is "in Christ."

Pure prayer cannot therefore be separated from participation in the sacramental life of the Church. "The Jesus prayer," comments O. Clement, "becomes the breath of the confident soul, the search for the place of the heart within becomes

transformed into love for Christ's own heart: and the blood
of the Eucharist is the guardian of the senses and of the
heart."[62] And Cabasilas: "Truly this Blood transforms the
heart into which it is poured into a sanctuary of God even
more beautiful than the temple of Solomon."[63]

When he describes the divine beauty and brilliance in
which Christians participate when in communion with the
light of the glorious Christ, Cabasilas is imbued with such
grace in his witness to the spiritual experience of the glory
of Christ that his description may well bear comparison with
the best pages of St. Gregory Palamas and St. Simeon the
New Theologian. For him, even more than for his predecessors, the baptismal and Eucharistic grace is the source of
the believer's illumination, and it is the flame proceeding
from the Eucharistic Mysteries which sets on fire the believer's
heart.

The fundamental belief of Palamas and the hesychasts
that the saints might after the manner of the Apostles contemplate the light of Christ on Mount Tabor with the eyes
of their transfigured bodies, permits them to safeguard the
reality of the divine life which is given us by the Church
through its mysteries. "Becoming one body with us," writes
Palamas, "and making of us a temple of his whole divinity
surely he will illuminate those who communicate worthily
with the divine ray of the Life-giving Body which is in
us, and will enlighten their souls as he enlightened even the
bodies of the disciples on Mount Tabor. For then that Body,
Source of light and grace, was not united to us and within
us, but enlightened from without those who approached
worthily, sending light through the medium of their bodily
eyes; but today as he is wholly one with us and within us,
he enlightens the soul from within."[64] So for Palamas this
illumination is the fruit of the sacramental union with the
Body of the Word Incarnate.[65] This sacramental context of
the transfiguration is even more clearly stated by Cabasilas
in pages which are unsurpassed for their inspiration in all
patristic literature and so justly deserve to be quoted.

Faithful to his sacramental vision, it is to the sacraments
that Cabasilas traces the gift of spiritual illumination.

"Through the intermediary of the sacraments as through a great opening the Sun of Righteousness shines into this dark world. . . . And the Light of the world conquers this world. . . . When the rays of the sun penetrate a room, this draws all eyes to them, and the light of the candle grows dim: so likewise the glory of the life to come, entering this world by the sacraments, triumphs in those souls over the earthly life and blots out the brilliance of this world."[66]

All the senses of man are transfigured and awakened by the light and power of grace. "The life of the world to come flows into the life here on earth and the Sun of celestial glory shines even on us with great compassion, and the heavenly perfume invades the earthly sphere, and the bread of angels is given to man."[67]

This illumination is above all a fruit of baptism. In all the baptismal catechisms of the Fathers, baptism is represented as Light:[68] "Awake, O sleeper, and arise from the dead, and Christ shall give you light" (Eph. 5:14), said St. Paul, probably quoting a primitive baptismal hymn, for it is also quoted by St. John Chrysostom. For St. Gregory Nazianzen, the baptismal light is one that renews all the senses: "May the baptismal light invade our eyes, ears, our sense of smell, in fact our whole body."[69]

"All the rites which accompany the baptismal ceremonies," Cabasilas will repeat, "symbolize precisely this very illumination, for the whole ceremony is a feast of lights; the lamp-stands, the canticles, the movement of the choirs, the triumphant ceremonial: there is nothing which does not overflow in joy, even the baptismal robes, white and shining, betoken those who will see the light."[70]

Cabasilas quotes freely and fully from St. John Chrysostom: "As soon as we are baptised our soul, purified by the Holy Spirit, is more glorious than the sun, and not only do we contemplate the glory of God, but we receive of its brilliance. . . ."[71] Even in the bodies of the saints the light of divine grace is reflected: "Nothing can compare with that interior glory—"the skin of Moses' face shone" (Ex. 34:35), but the saints carry this light within their souls with even more brilliance; for the shining forth in Moses belongs to the senses, that of the Apostles was of the spirit. These luminosities coming from bodies full of light are spread abroad on surrounding objects which reflect their light: so it is with faithful souls. This is why souls thus blessed desire no more of things earthly but dream only of heaven."[72]

But this vision is not lasting for "we allow ourselves to be seduced by things of the earth; this ineffable and unspeakable glory remains with us for a day or two: and then we extinguish it by introducing within us the whirl of secularity and blot out the rays by a thick cloud."[73] This complaint of St. John Chrysostom Cabasilas makes his own and even underlines it. "You will misunderstand me if you believe that this swift illumination infuses into the soul an habitual awareness of God, or a peaceful illumination of the mind. This light will be extinguished in one or two days in the midst of anything that is agitated or tumultuous."[74]

This germ of immortal life and divine light received in baptism must grow and bring forth fruit. This is the work of the Holy Spirit. It is in the partaking of the Eucharistic feast that the baptismal illumination will attain to its fulness on earth.

Following in the steps of St. Cyril of Alexandria[75] and St. Simeon the New Theologian,[76] Nicholas Cabasilas will take up the symbol of fire and unite it with light so that the soul becomes in its turn full of light. "When the presence of the Divine Guest invades the whole dwelling of the soul, it is he himself in his fulness that we possess and not some special gift: we do not receive some rays of light but the Sun of Righteousness himself."[77]

The liturgical meditations on the love of Christ teach us to venerate him who has loved us with an everlasting love, "to entrust our souls to him, to dedicate our lives to him, to enkindle in our hearts the flame of his love. Thus prepared we can enter into contact with the glowing Fire of the Solemn Mysteries with confidence and trust."[78] And a little farther on in the *Commentary on the Divine Liturgy*, Ch. I, he says: "In this way adding sanctification to sanctification, that of the sacred rite to that of the meditations, we are changed into his likeness from 'one degree of glory to another' (2 Cor. 3:18); that is from the lesser glory to that which is the greatest of all."[79]

This liturgical and Eucharistic experience of light, of a Cabasilas or a Palamas, cannot truly be understood except in the eschatological perspective which is inherent to it. The vision of Christ transfigured is understood by the Eastern Fathers as an anticipation of the glorious and fearful coming of Christ. "It is in the glory of the Father," says Palamas, "that the righteous will shine like the sun in the kingdom of their Father . . . (Matt. 13:43); they will be all light and they will see the Light, a wonderful and holy sight belonging only to the pure in heart. Today this light shines in part, as a promise for those who in stillness have overcome all that is evil and by pure spiritual prayer all that is impure; but in that day this light will deify in an open way the sons of the resurrection (Lk. 20:36), who will rejoice in an eternity of glory in communion with him who has imparted to human nature a glory and divine brilliance."[80]

The human body nourished by the Eucharistic bread during its earthly life, quickened by the Holy Spirit and enlightened with celestial light, "even this dust," according to Cabasilas, "will show forth all its beauty as a member of this light, will be conformed to this Sun and will give forth similar rays of light. . . . In that day the righteous will shine with the same brilliance and the same glory as Christ, they in joy to receive from him, he to impart to them that brilliance and glory. For this Bread, this Body that they will take with them into life eternal having been nourished at the Eucharistic table here below, this is the Lord Christ who will appear to all men in the clouds, who will manifest his splendour to the East and to the West in a flash in a moment of time."[81] "It is thus glorified that the righteous live here on earth; at their death this glory will not leave them. The just carry always within them this light and glory and they will take it with them into the new life and hasten towards him to whom they have never ceased to be united."[82]

In a final evocation of the glory of the Christ Pantocrator and of our transfiguration in him, Nicholas Cabasilas describes in unforgettable words the glory which will clothe the servants of God. "Then," he cries, "each one of us can shed forth rays brighter than those of the sun, rise above the clouds, see this body of God, rise towards him, fly towards him . . . come near and contemplate him in peace." And Cabasilas transports us in thought to that glorious assembly of the elect in the heavenly country. "A solemnity, unsurpassed! A whole people of gods around their God, of beautiful creatures around him who is the Beautiful, of servants around their Master. . . . The choir of the elect, the company of the blessed. . . . Such dazzling wonder descends from the skies to earth, and suns in their turn will rise from earth to glorify the Sun of Righteousness himself . . . all is flooded with Light."[83]

Overflowing paschal joy . . . this is the final message of our Byzantine master who says with St. Paul, "If we suffer with him we shall also reign with him" (2 Tim. 2:12).

CONCLUSION

It is Cabasilas by his own words who has guided us, as we have explored the development of the rich spirituality traditional in the Christian East. Another work often misunderstood but authentically hesychastic, on the love which is aflame for Christ, is that of St. Simeon the New Theologian, Abbot of St. Mamas, the same monastery where John Cantacuzene and Nicholas Cabasilas had intended to retire. The hymns of St. Simeon on the divine "Eros" are a unique expression of the meeting and colloquy of the soul with Christ, now ecstatic, now painful, now in an intimacy almost unbearable, now on the contrary in abandonment and darkness. Nearly four centuries before palamism, St. Simeon lived the overwhelming experience of the uncreated light of the grace of God which invaded and satisfied his soul unceasingly.

> Light simple and to be adored,
> Light which at times hides itself, at times unites itself
> Wholly, as it seems to me, to us, your servants.
> Light spiritually contemplated from afar,
> Light suddenly revealed within us.

Light sometimes like to fire which kindles,
Sometimes to running water. . . .
My humble and tormented soul is on fire—
It is on fire, and flames.[84]

"It is incontestable," writes M. Lot-Borodine, "that the experience of St. Simeon which stirred and inspired the souls of men, prepared the way for the renewal of the mysticism of the 14th century. . . . Such a soul on fire must, by its ardent quest for contact between man and God, as well as by the felt quality of its experience, have had a strong effect on Nicholas Cabasilas athirst with a similar desire. This even more because St. Simeon had given his heart irrevocably to the Person of Christ, who is Word of God, Master, Beloved. It will be from this burning hearth that will fly that spark that will enlighten and feed the love, the "eros" of Cabasilas."[85]

The golden chain of souls which have been illuminated and transfigured by the fire of Christ's love passes on from St. Simeon to Palamas and Cabasilas, and to the masters of Byzantine spirituality down to our own day. The incomparable charismatic grace given to Nicholas was to enable him to find words and expressions to describe the vision of theologians and mystics in a language that could be understood, and in a context which could be realized in the world. He proclaimed the universality not only of faith and the common evangelical morality, but of the immediacy of the call of Christ to perfection and of the urgency of the response of man by a total gift of himself to that insatiable love of the Master.

Cabasilas was able to say in fresh words and with irresistible conviction that the life in Christ, sought in the silence of the cloister and in solitude, by pure prayer, by the purification of the passions, by the forsaking of the world and its preoccupations, that this very same life is communicated in its fulness to all Christians. Through the Eucharist "they live now this life in Christ,"[86] are endowed with a royal dignity, are assimilated to Christ by the Bread of Life, and "transformed by his Blood into a sanctuary more beautiful than the temple of Solomon."[87]

INTRODUCTION NOTES

[1]M. Lot-Borodine, *Un maître de la spiritualité byzantine: Nicolas Cabasilas,* Editions de l'Orante (Paris: 1958), p. 5. Henceforth referred to as *L.B.*

[2]In his introduction to the German translation of *The Life in Christ,* "Sakramentalmystik der Ostkirche, das Buch vom Leben in Christo des Nikolaus Kabasilas" (Munich: 1957), pp. 5-13.

[3]B. Tatakis, *La philosophie byzantine* (Paris: 1949), pp. 277-81.

[4]Ed. A. Garzya, in *Byzantion* 24 (1954), pp. 521-537.

[5]*A Study of Gregory Palamas* (London: 1964), p. 25.

[6]*The Life in Christ,* Book VI. P.G. 150, col. 681 AB. (Henceforth referred to as V.C.); cf. abr. VC. 584 C and 620 D-621 A.

[7]Cf. *A Study,* p. 102.

[8]Ibid., p. 394 (in the French edition).

[9]Ibid., pp. 396-7 (in the French edition). Dom P. Miguel in his article "L'expérience sacramentelle selon Nicolas Cabasilas" in *Irenikon,* 28 (1965), No. 2, pp. 176-82, makes a decided opposition between the "extra-sacramental atmosphere" of the great mystics and particularly Gregory Palamas on the one hand, and on the other the sacramental experience which is fostered and developed according to Cabasilas through the reception of the Sacraments. This contrast seems to us to be exaggerated. This view of palamite "mysticism" does not stand up to a careful reading of his homilies (cf. further section 2 of this article).

[10]L.B., p. 180.

[11]V.C. 657 D-660 A.

[12]V.C. 664 A.B.

[13]V.C. 681 B.

[14]Ps. Denis, Ecclesiachies. P.G. 3, 504 C. Scholiae of Maximus the Confessor. P.G. 4, 136 A.

[15]Confessio Fidei, P.G. 151, 766-7.

[16]V.C. 684 C.

[17]V.C. 585 A.

[18]V.C. 585 B.

[19]V.C. 593 BC.

[20]Hom. 56, ed. Oikonomos (Athens: 1861), pp. 206-8 quoted by Meyendorff, pp. 177-8.

[21]V.C. 584 C.

[22]V.C. 593 A.B.

[23]V.C. 597 D-600 A.

[24]V.C. 601 C.

[25]L.B., p. 114.

[26]V.C. 584 D.

[27]Hom. 15, 20. P.G. 34, col. 589 B.

[28]Step 27. P.G. 88, 1096ff.

[29]Cf. Meyendorff, *A Study*, pp. 137-8.

[30]Ibid., p. 152.

[31]V.C. 596 D-597 B.

[32]V.C. 601 D.

[33]V.C. 612 C.D.

[34]V.C. 617 B.

[35]V.C. 620 B.C.

[36]V.C. 621 B.

[37]V.C. 625. B.

[38]*Commentary,* Chap. 36. P.G. 150, 449 A, E. T. Hussey and McNutty (henceforth H.M.), p. 89.

[39]Ibid. P.G. 452 C.D. H.M., p. 91.

[40]Ibid. P.G. 452 D-453 A. H.M., pp. 91-2.

[41]Ibid. P.G. 453 A. H.M., p. 92.

[42]L.B., p. 115.

[43]Cf. Salaville, *Explication de la divine liturgie,* Sources chrétiennes 4 (Paris: 1943), pp. 44-5, 59-60.

[44]L.B., p. 21, note.

[45]V.C. 652.

[46]V.C. 605 A.

[47]V.C. 605 C.

[48]V.C. 608 AB.

[49]V.C. 656 D.

[50]V.C. 645 A.

[51]V.C. 641 C.D.

[52]V.C. 644 A.B.

[53]L.B., pp. 129-32.

[54]Ibid., p. 130.

[55]Ibid., p. 130.

[56]The Pastor of Hermas, parab. 9. 14.

[57]V.C. 681 D. 684 A.

[58]V.C. 681 B.

[59]V.C. 685 C.

[60]*A Study*, p. 140.

[61]V.C. 684 A.

[62]*Byzance et Christianisme* (Paris: 1964), p. 62.

[63]V.C. 685 C.

[64]*Triades pour la défense des saints hesychastes,* 1. 3. 38, ed. J. Meyendorff (Louvain: 1959), p. 192.

[65]Cf. *A Study*, p. 161.

[66]V.C. 504 B.C.

[67]V.C. 496 C.D.

[68]See: J. Danielou, "Le Symbolisme des rites baptismaux," in *Dieu Vivant*, I (1945), p. 36; L.B., pp. 85-8 (on sacramental baptism and baptism of blood in Nicholas Cabasilas); and Hamman, *Le baptême d'après les Pères de l'Eglise* (Paris: 1962), pp. 19-21.

[69]Ibid., p. 142.

[70]V.C. 565 B.

[71]V.C. 564 B.

[72]V.C. 564 C.D.

[73]V.C. 564 D-565 A. Br. 82-3, and St. John Chrysostom, Hom. 7 in 2 Cor. P.G. 61, 448.

[74]V.C. 565 A.

[75]St. Cyril compares the sacred flesh of Christ to "the fire which penetrates cold matter and makes it burn," and to "the spark which falls into the straw and burns it up" (quoted in L.B., p. 104).

[76]The Eucharistic prayers of St. Symeon contained in manuals of Orthodox prayers speak the same overwhelming language. Cf. O. Clement, *L'essor du christianisme oriental* (Paris: 1964), pp. 33-4.

[77]V.C. 584 D. Br. 100.

[78]*Commentary*, Chap. 1. P.G. 150, 373 D. H.M., p. 29.

[79]Ibid., 376 B. H.M., p. 30.

[80]*Triades*, 11, 33, 66. See other texts of Palamas in *A Study*, p. 174; and the works of V. Lossky, "La théologie de la lumière chez S. Gregoire Palamas," in Dieu Vivant, I (1945), pp. 107-10, and *The Vision of God* (London: 1965), pp. 124-37.

[81]V.C. 624 A.B.

[82]V.C. 624 B.; cf. *Commentary*, cp. 43. P.G. 150, 461-4. H.M., pp. 98-100.

[83]V.C. 649 B.D.

[84]Quoted in L.B., p. 182.

[85]L.B., pp. 183-4.

[86]*Commentary*, cp. 36 and 38. P.G. 150, 449 C and 453 A. H.M., pp. 88-92.

[87]V.C. 684 C.

THE FIRST BOOK

How the life in Christ is constituted by means of the divine Mysteries of Baptism, Chrismation, and Holy Communion

[§ 1.   How the life in Christ begins in this life]

The life in Christ originates in this life and arises from it. It is perfected, however, in the life to come, when we shall have reached that last day. It cannot attain perfection in men's souls in this life, nor even in that which is to come without already having begun here. Since that which is carnal, the mist and corruption which derive from the flesh, cannot inherit incorruption (1 Cor. 15:50), it casts a shadow over that life in this present time. Therefore Paul thought it to be a great advantage to depart in order to be with Christ, for he says, "to depart and to be with Christ is far better" (Phil. 1:23). But if the life to come were to admit those who lack the faculties and senses necessary for it, it would avail nothing for their happiness, but they would be dead and miserable living in that blessed and immortal world. The reason is, that the light would appear and the sun shine with its pure rays with no eye having been formed to see it. The Spirit's fragrance would be abundantly diffused and pervading all, but one would not know it without already having the sense of smell.

Now it is possible for the Son of God to make His friends to share in His Mysteries* in preparation for that day, and for them to learn from Him what He has heard from the Father (Jn. 15:15). But they must come as His friends who "have ears to hear" (Mt. 11:15). Then it is impossible to begin the friendship and to open the ear, to prepare the wedding garment and to make ready the other requisites for that bridechamber; it is this life which is the workshop for all these things. Those, then, who have not acquired these things before they departed have nothing in common with that life. To this the five foolish virgins and the man invited to the wedding feast are witnesses, since they came without either the oil or the wedding garment and were not able to buy them then.

[§ 2. The life in Christ consists of union with Him]

In short, it is this world which is in travail with that new inner man which is "created after the likeness of God" (Eph. 4:24). When he has been shaped and formed here he is thus born perfect into that perfect world which grows not old. As nature prepares the foetus, while it is in its dark and fluid life, for that life which is in the light, and shapes it, as though according to a model, for the life which it is about to receive, so likewise it happens to the saints. This is what the apostle Paul said when he wrote to the Galatians, "my little children, with whom I am again in travail until Christ be formed in you" (Gal. 4:19).

However, while the unborn have no perception whatever of this life, the blessed ones have many hints in this present life of things to come. This is the reason. The unborn do not yet possess this life, but it is wholly in the future. In that condition there is no ray of light nor anything else which sustains this life. In our case this is not so, but that future life is, as it were, infused into this present life and

---

*I.e., Sacraments.

mingled with it. For us too that Sun has graciously risen, the heavenly fragrance has been poured forth into the malodorous places, and the Bread of angels has been given even to men.

In this present world, therefore, it is possible for the saints not only to be disposed and prepared for that life, but also even now to live and act in accordance with it. Paul writes, "lay hold on eternal life" (Tim. 6:12), and "it is no longer I who live, but Christ who lives in me" (Gal. 2:20). The divine Ignatius says, "there is water living and speaking in me" (To the Romans, 7:2). Scripture is full of such passages! Beside all these, when He who is the Life promises the saints to be with them for ever, and says, "behold, I am with you always, to the close of the age" (Mt. 28:20), what else should one think? When He had sown the seed of life on the earth (Lk. 8:5) and cast on it the fire (Lk. 12:49) and the sword (Mt. 10:34), He did not forthwith depart and leave it to men to plant and nourish the seed and to kindle the fire and use the sword. He Himself is truly with us and "works in us to will and to do, as the blessed Paul said (Phil. 2:12). It is He Himself who kindles and applies the fire, He Himself holds the sword. In short, "neither does the axe boast without him who lifts it" (Is. 10:15). Those from whom the Good One is absent will attain to no good.

Yet the Lord did not promise merely to be present with the saints, but to abide with them—nay more than this, to make His abode in them (Jn. 14:23). What then shall I say? Where it is said that He is united with them, it is with such love that He becomes one spirit with them. As Paul says, "he who is united to the Lord becomes one spirit with Him" (I Cor. 6:17), and "that you may be one body and one spirit, just as you were called" (Eph. 4:4).

[§ 3.   The intimacy of our union with Christ]

As God's loving-kindness is ineffable and His love for our race surpasses human speech and reason, so too it

belongs to the divine goodness alone, for this is "the peace
of God which passes all understanding" (Phil. 4:7). Likewise
it follows that His union with those whom He loves surpasses
every union of which one might conceive, and cannot be
compared with any model.

Therefore even Scripture needed many illustrations to
be able to express that connection, since one would not
suffice. In one place it employs the figures of an inhabitant
and a dwelling, in another those of a vine and a branch,
here that of a marriage, there that of members and a head.
None of those figures is adequate for that union, for it
is impossible from these to attain to the exact truth.
Above all it is necessary that the union should conform to
friendship—yet what could be adequate for divine love?

It would appear that marriage and the concord between
head and members especially indicate connection and unity,
yet they fall far short of it and are far from manifesting
the reality. Marriage does not so join together that those
who are united exist and live in each other, as is the case
with Christ and the Church. So the divine apostle, speaking
of marriage, says, "this is a great mystery," and adds, "I
speak of Christ and the Church" (Eph. 5:32), showing that
it is not marriage, but union with Christ which he sets up
for admiration. The members are joined to the head; they
are alive because they are joined and die if they are
separated. But it appears that the members of Christ are
more closely joined to Him than to their own head, and
that it is even more by Him that they live than by their
concord with it. This is plain from the blessed martyrs,
who gladly suffered the one (i.e., dismemberment of their
bodies) but would not even hear of the other, for they gave
up their heads and limbs with pleasure, but could not even
by word revolt from Christ.

So I come to that which is strangest. To whom else
could one be more closely united than to oneself? Yet this
very unity is inferior to that union. For each of the spirits
of the blessed ones is identical with himself, yet it is united
to the Saviour more than to him. It loves the Saviour more
than itself, and of this Paul will bear witness by the saying

in which he wishes that he were "anathema from Christ
for the sake of the salvation of the Jews" (Rom. 9:13) so
that it might redound to His greater glory. But if human
love is so great, the divine love is inconceivable. If the
wicked can show so great gratitude, what ought to be said
of God's goodness? Since the love is so immense, the union
in which it has joined those who love must needs so surpass
man's understanding that it cannot be likened to any
similitude whatever.

[§ 4. **In this union Christ is all-sufficient**]

Let us then examine it in this way. There are many
things of which we stand in need throughout life—such as
air, light, food, clothing, our natural faculties and members;
yet it so happens that we do not use any of them constantly
for all purposes. We use one of them at one time, another
at another time, each in turn helping us to meet the need
which is at hand. When we put on clothing it cannot feed
us, those who need nourishment must seek something else.
The light does not enable us to breathe; the air cannot take
the place of a ray of light. We do not constantly employ
all the functions of our senses and members, but from
time to time the eye and the hand are idle, as when we
have to listen. The hand will suffice for those who wish
to touch, but not for smelling or hearing or seeing; for
those purposes we ignore it and look to some other faculty.
But in such a way the Saviour is ever present in every
fashion with those who dwell in Him, that He supplies their
every need and is all things to them, nor does He suffer
them to look to anything else whatever nor seek anything
from elsewhere. There is nothing of which the saints are in
need which He is not Himself. He gives them birth, growth,
and nourishment; He is life and breath. By means of Himself
He forms an eye for them and, in addition, gives them light
and enables them to see Himself. He is the one who feeds
and is Himself the Food; it is He who provides the Bread
of life and who is Himself what He provides. He is life

for those who live, the sweet odour to those who breathe, the garment for those who would be clothed. Indeed, He is the One who enables us to walk; He Himself is the way (Jn. 14:6), and in addition He is the lodging on the way and its destination. We are members, He is the head. When we must struggle He struggles on our side. For those who are champions in the contest He is the awarder of the prizes; when we are the victors He is the crown of victory.

Thus He turns our mind to Himself from every side and does not permit it to occupy itself with anything else nor to be seized by love of anything else. Even though we move our desire in another direction, He checks it and quiets it. He blocks that way and takes in hand those who go astray. "If I go up into heaven, thou art there," it says, "if I go down to hell, thou art there also. If I take up my wings in the morning, and dwell in the uttermost parts of the sea, even there also shall thy hand lead me, and thy right hand shall hold me" (Ps. 139:8-10). By a wondrous compulsion and gracious governance He draws us to Himself alone and unites us to Himself only. This, I think, is the same compulsion by which He gathered those whom He invited to the house and the banquet when He said to the servant, "Compel them to come in, that my house may be filled (Lk. 14:23).

[§ 5.   We attain to this union by newness of life]

So then, from what has been said it is clear that the life in Christ is present to the saints, those who live and work in accordance with it, not only in the world to come but also in that which is here and now. But how it is possible to live in this way and, as Paul says, "walk in newness of life" (Rom. 6:4), and further, what it is that they do with whom Christ is thus united and grown together—and I know not how else to describe it—must be discussed in that which follows.

There is an element which derives from God, and another which derives from our own zeal. The one is entirely His work, the other involves striving on our part.

However, the latter is our contribution only to the extent that we submit to His grace and do not surrender the treasure nor extinguish the torch when it has been lighted. By this I mean that we contribute nothing which is either hostile to the life or produces death. It is to this that all human good and every virtue leads, that no one should draw the sword against himself, nor flee from happiness, nor toss the crowns of victory from off his head. When Christ Himself is present He implants the very essence of life into our souls in an ineffable manner, for He is truly present and as He by His coming has supplied the first principles of life, so He assists their growth. He is present, however, not as when He first came to share our conditions of life, our company, and our pursuits, but in a different and more perfect way, in that we are joined to Him in the same body and share His life and are His members.

So, just as it is a wondrous loving-kindness which impelled Him so to love those who were the basest and to count them worthy of the greatest favours, so the union by which He is present with the objects of His love surpasses every image and every name. Thus too the manner in which He is present and bestows His benefits is a marvellous one, worthy of Him alone who does wondrous things. Those who imitate, as it were by a picture, by means of certain signs and symbols, the death which He truly died for the sake of our life, He renews and recreates by these very acts and makes them partakers of His own life.

[§ 6.   Christ bestows this new life through His Mysteries]

In the sacred Mysteries, then, we depict His burial and proclaim His death. By them we are begotten and formed and wondrously united to the Saviour, for they are the means by which, as Paul says, "in Him we live, and move, and have our being" (Acts 17:28).

Baptism confers being and in short, existence according to Christ. It receives us when we are dead and corrupted

and first leads us into life. The anointing with chrism
perfects him who has received [new] birth by infusing
into him the energy that befits such a life. The Holy
Eucharist preserves and continues this life and health, since
the Bread of life enables us to preserve that which has been
acquired and to continue in life. It is therefore by this Bread
that we live and by the chrism that we are moved, once we
have received being from the baptismal washing.

In this way we live in God. We remove our life
from this visible world to that world which is not seen by
exchanging, not the place, but the very life itself and its
mode. It was not we ourselves who were moved towards
God, nor did we ascend to Him; but it was He who came
and descended to us. It was not we who sought, but we
were the object of His seeking. The sheep did not seek for
the shepherd, nor did the lost coin search for the master of
the house; He it was who came to the earth and retrieved
His own image, and He came to the place where the sheep
was straying and lifted it up and stopped it from straying.
He did not remove us from here, but He made us heavenly
while yet remaining on earth and imparted to us the
heavenly life without leading us up to heaven, but by
bending heaven to us and bringing it down. As the prophet
says, "He bowed the heavens also, and came down" (Ps.
18:10).

Accordingly, through these sacred Mysteries as through
windows the Sun of Righteousness enters this dark world.
He puts to death the life which accords with this world,
but raises up that which is above the world. The Light of
the world overcomes this world, which He affirms when
He says, "I have overcome the world" (Jn. 16:33), and
introduces the abiding and immortal life into a mortal body
which is subject to change.

When the sunlight enters a house the lamp no longer
attracts the sight of the onlookers, but the brightness
of the sunlight overcomes it and dims it. Similarly, when in
this life the brightness of the life to come enters through
the Mysteries and dwells in our souls it overcomes the life
which is in the flesh and the beauty of this world and

conceals their brightness. This is the life which is in the
Spirit, which overcomes every desire of the flesh in accordance
with Paul's word, "walk by the Spirit, and do not gratify
the desires of the flesh" (Gal. 5:16). This way the Lord
traced by coming to us, this gate He opened by entering into
the world. When He returned to the Father He suffered it
not to be closed, but from Him He comes through it to
sojourn among men, or rather, He is constantly present with
us and, in fulfilment of those promises, is with us for ever.
Therefore, as the patriarch said, "this is none other but the
house of God, and this is the gate of heaven" (Gen. 28:17).
By it not only the angels descend to the earth, for they are
present with each one who is being initiated, but even the
very Lord of the angels Himself.

Accordingly, when He prefigured, as by a picture, our
own Baptism, the Saviour Himself as He suffered Himself
to undergo the baptism of John opened up heaven and
showed that this is the means by which we shall see the
heavenly place. Indeed, the words in which He declared that
he who has not been baptized will not be able to enter into
life (Jn. 3:5) hint that this washing is some kind of
entrance and gate. "Open to me the gates of righteousness"
(Ps. 118:19), says David, moved by desire that these gates
should be opened. That which many prophets and kings
desired to see (Lk. 10:24) is this, that the Artificer of
those doors should come to the earth. Therefore David
states that were he to attain to this entrance and go through
these gates he would render thanks to God who has breached
the wall, for he says, "I will go into them and give thanks
unto the Lord" (Ps. 118:19), since it is from these gates
that he would be able to attain to the most perfect knowledge
of the goodness and loving-kindness of God towards our
race.

What then could be a greater proof of kindness and
benevolence than that He who washes with water should
set the soul free from uncleanness? Or that He by anointing
it with chrism should grant it to reign in the heavenly
kingdom? Or that He as the Host of the banquet should
provide His own Body and Blood? And moreover, that men

should become gods (cf. Jn. 10:35) and sons of God (cf. Rom. 8:14). And that our nature should be honoured with God's honour, and that dust should be raised to such a height of glory as to become equal in honour and dignity to the divine nature?

This, then, is the excellence of God's work which has beclouded the very heavens. It has surpassed, I think, every creature and concealed every other work of God by excelling it in greatness and beauty. All of God's works, be they ever so many, so beautiful, and so great, are less than the Creator's wisdom and skill so that He could well have brought forward things yet more beautiful and yet greater than those which already exist, such as we should not be able to express. But were it possible for a work of God to take place, so beautiful, so great that it would vie with that wisdom and power, and almost match His infinity and, like a footprint, indicate the whole greatness of His divine goodness, I should regard this to be superior to the others. If, then, God's work always consists in imparting goodness, it is for this end that He does all things. This is the goal both of past events and of things which may happen in time to come, since "the good has been poured forth and spreads abroad" (Dionysius, *Of the Divine Names,* c. 4). By doing this God would impart the greatest good of all. Greater than this He could not give, and this would be the greatest and fairest work of His goodness and the utmost limit of His kindness.

Such, then, is the work of that dispensation which was wrought for mankind. In this case God did not merely impart whatever was good for human nature and keep most for Himself, but He bestowed all the "fulness of His Godhead" (Col. 2:9), all the riches of His very nature. It was for this reason that Paul said that in the Gospel the righteousness of God is eminently revealed (Rom. 1:17). For if there is any virtue and righteousness of God it would consist in bountifully imparting to all His own excellence and in sharing His blessedness.

For this reason the most sacred Mysteries may fittingly be called "gates of righteousness," for it is God's supreme

loving-kindness and goodness towards mankind, which is
the divine virtue and righteousness, which has provided us
with these entrances into heaven.

[§ 7.   Christ's saving work as the foundation of the new life]

In yet another way, by an act of judgment and
righteousness, the Lord has set up this sign of triumph
and has given us this gate and this way. He did not steal
away the captives, but gave a ransom for them. He bound
"the strong man" (Mk. 3:27), not by virtue of greater
power, but by condemning him with a just sentence. He
became king over the house of Jacob by destroying the
tyrant's dominion in men's souls, not merely because He
was able to destroy it, but because it deserved to be destroyed.
This he pointed out by the saying, "Righteousness and
justice are the foundation of thy throne" (Ps. 89:14).

It was not merely that righteousness opened those gates,
but that through them righteousness reached our race. In
times past, before God had sojourned among men, it was
impossible to find righteousness upon the earth. God, from
whom nothing is hid, Himself stooped down from heaven
and sought it, to see whether it existed at all; yet He did
not find it, for He says, "they are all gone out of the way,
they are altogether unprofitable, there is none that doeth
good, no, not one" (Ps. 14:4, LXX).

But when the truth rose, like the sun, from the earth
for those who sat in the darkness and shadow of falsehood,
then righteousness stooped down from heaven and, for the
first time, appeared to men in its reality and perfection. We
were justified, first by being set free from bonds and
condemnation, in that He who had done no evil pleaded
for us by dying on the cross. By this He paid the penalty
for the sins which we had audaciously committed; then,
because of that death, we were made friends of God and
righteous. By His death the Saviour not only released us
and reconciled us to the Father, but also "gave us power to

become children of God" (Jn. 1:12), in that He both united
our nature to Himself through the flesh which He assumed,
and also united each one of us to His own flesh by the
power of the Mysteries.

In this way, then, He makes His own righteousness and
life to rise, like the sun, in our souls. Thus it became
possible for men, by means of the sacred Mysteries, both to
know true righteousness and themselves to practice it.

[§ 8. How the righteous under the Old Covenant looked forward to their deliverance by Christ]

Even though in Scripture there were many righteous
men and friends of God before the coming of the Justifier
and Reconciler, we ought to consider this both in the
particular context of their own generation and also with
reference to that which was to come. It was for this that
they were enabled and prepared, that when righeousness
should appear they would run towards it, and that when
the ransom would be paid they would be released; that
when the light would shine they would see it, and when
the reality had been disclosed they would rise above the
types and shadows.

While the righteous and the wicked were held by almost
the same bonds and endured the same tyranny, yet they
differed in this respect, that the righteous hated that
captivity and slavery. They prayed that their prison might
be destroyed and those bonds broken, they wished to see
the tyrant's head trampled under foot by those who had
been his captives. The wicked, on the other hand, by no
means regarded their present plight as a calamity and were
happy to be slaves. Such were they also who, at that blessed
time when the Sun had risen upon them, did not accept it,
but sought by every means to extinguish it and did all they
could to cause the sunlight to vanish. When, therefore, the
King appeared, the former were set free from the tyranny
of hell, while the latter remained in their bonds.

In the case of the sick, those who in every way seek for

healing and gladly see the physician are in a better and more tolerable case than those who do not even know that they are sick and who shrink from medicines. The physician who knows that his art is equal to the disease will, I think, address them as though they have already recovered, even though he has not yet cured them. It was in this sense that God called men both righteous and friends in those times, for they made every effort in their power and displayed such righteousness as was possible.

This made them worthy of being released when He should appear who had the power to release them, yet He by no means released them beforehand. Had this been true righteousness then they, as Solomon says, should have been "in peace" and "in the hand of God" (Wis. 3:1, 3) when they had laid aside this body, but it was Hades that received them when they had departed hence. When our Master brought in true righteousness and fellowship with God it was not as though He brought them back from abroad; He brought them into the world for the first time. He did not discover an already existing road leading to heaven, He Himself was its builder. Had it already existed, someone else would have built it, but now "no one has ascended into heaven but He who descended from heaven, the Son of man" (Jn. 3:13).

Since, then, it was impossible to find forgiveness of sins and remission of punishment before the cross, what must we think of righteousness? It would not have been consistent, I think, for the just to be placed with the choir of God's friends before being reconciled to Him, or to be proclaimed as receiving the crowns of victory while they were still bound in chains. In short, had the passover lamb of the Old Covenant accomplished all things, what need would there have been for the second paschal Victim? Had the types and the images brought about the felicity which was being sought after, the truth and realities would have been in vain. Since the enmity was destroyed through Christ's death and the dividing wall removed (Eph. 2:14, 16), and since peace and righteousness rose as the sun in the days of the Saviour, would there have been any place

for all these things if there had been friends of God and
righteous men before that sacrifice?

Here is a further proof. Formerly it was the law which
united us to God, but now it is faith and grace and all
that depends on them. It is thus clear that at that time the
fellowship of men with God was a condition of servitude,
but that it is now one of sonship and friendship, for the
law pertains to slaves, but grace, confidence, and faith
belong to friends and sons. From all these things it is
obvious that since the Saviour is "the first-born from the
dead" (Col. 1:18) so it was not possible for anyone of the
dead to revive to immortal life before He had risen. In
the same way too He alone led the way to holiness and
righteousness for mankind. This Paul showed when he
wrote that Christ "has gone as a forerunner for us" into
the Holy Place (Heb. 6:20). He entered into the Holy
Place when He had offered Himself to the Father, and He
leads in those who are willing, as they share in His burial.
This, however, does not consist in dying as He died, but in
showing forth that death in the baptismal washing and
proclaiming it upon the sacred table, when they, after being
anointed, in an ineffable manner feast upon Him who was
done to death and rose again. Thus, when He has led them
through the gates, He brings them to the kingdom and the
crowns.

[§ 9.   How Christ opens to us the gates of life]

The gates of the Mysteries are far more august and
beneficial than the gates of Paradise. The latter will not be
opened to anyone who has not first entered through the
gates of the Mysteries, but these were opened when the
gates of Paradise had been closed. The latter were able to
let out those who were within, while the former only lead
inside and let no one out. It was possible to shut the gates
of Paradise and so they were shut; in the case of the
Mysteries the curtain and the dividing wall were entirely
destroyed and taken away. It is impossible to raise a barrier

anew and for the gates to be closed again and these worlds to be divided from each other by a wall. For "the heavens were" not merely opened, but "parted asunder," as says the admirable Mark (1:10), showing that a door and entrance way and curtain no longer existed. He who has reconciled and united the world which is above with that which is below, and has made peace between them and destroyed the dividing wall (Eph. 2:14, 15), "cannot deny Himself," as blessed Paul says (2 Tim. 2:13).

The gates of Paradise were opened for Adam, but it was fitting that they be closed when he fell from the state in which he ought to have remained. These gates Christ Himself opened, "who committed no sin" (1 Pet. 2:22) and cannot sin, for as it says, "His righteousness remaineth for ever" (Ps. 111:3). Wherefore they must of necessity remain open and lead to life, but without providing a way out of life, for "I came," says the Saviour, "that they might have life" (Jn. 10:10). This is the life which the Lord came to bring, that those who come through these Mysteries should be partakers of His death and share in His passion. Apart from this it is impossible to escape death. It is not possible for him who has not been "baptized in water and the Spirit" (Jn. 3:5) to enter into life, nor can those who have not eaten the Flesh of the Son of man and drunk His Blood have life in themselves (Jn. 6:24).

[§ 10.   The Ransom which Christ has paid for us]

Let us examine this further. It is not possible for those who have not died to sin to live for God. So it is of God alone to be able to slay sin. For men it was necessary, for had we been defeated against our will we should have been worthy of retrieving our defeat; but for those who had become slaves of sin it was in no way possible. How should we have been able to prevail over that to which we had become slaves? Even had we been more powerful, yet "the slave is not greater than the master" (Mt. 10:24).

It was man, then, who by rights should have attained

this end and for whom it was fit to win the victory; but he had become enslaved by those whom he should have conquered in battle. God, however, who was indebted to no one, had the power to do these things. Therefore, as long as neither God nor man undertook the battle, sin lived on. It was impossible for the sun of the true life to rise on us, since it was man who should wrest the victory for himself but only God who was able to do so. It was necessary, therefore, for manhood to be joined to Deity, and for one and the same to possess the nature both of him to whom the warfare pertained and of Him who was able to prevail in it.

It is this, then, that comes about. God makes His own the struggle on behalf of the human race, for He becomes man. Man, being pure from all sin, overcomes sin, for He is God. In this way human nature is cleared of disgrace and, now that sin has fallen, puts on the crown of victory.

Even though it has not yet happened that each member of the human race has been victorious because of this, or has even entered into the struggle, yet he has been released from these bonds. This the Saviour Himself accomplished by means of the nature which He assumed. Thereby He gave to each member of humanity the power to slay sin and to share with Him in the hero's prize. Since after that victory He had to receive His crown and celebrate His triumph, He underwent wounds, the cross, and death, and as Paul says, "for the joy that was set before Him He endured the cross, despising the shame" (Heb. 12:2). What does this mean? He had done no wrong for which He might pay the penalty, nor had He committed sin, nor had He done anything of which the most shameless informer might accuse Him. Yet wounds, pain, and death were from the beginning devised against sin! Why then did the Lord permit it, since He loves man? It is not reasonable for goodness to take pleasure in an atrocity and in death. This is the reason that God permitted death and pain as soon as sin had entered in, not so much to inflict a penalty on the guilty but rather to supply a remedy for him who had fallen into sickness. Since, therefore, it was impossible to apply this penalty to the things which Christ had done, and since the Saviour had no trace of any disease for which He needed a remedy to heal Him, the power of His cup is applied to us and slays the sin that is in us. The wounding of Him who is under no censure becomes the penalty of those who are guilty of many things.

Since it was a great and wondrous penalty which more than outweighed the evils committed by men, it not only cancelled the indictment but added so great an abundance of benefits that He ascended into heaven in order to make those who were of the earth, the most hateful captives, enslaved and dishonoured, to become partakers with God of the heavenly kingdom. That death was precious beyond the power of human thought, and yet the Saviour yielded Himself to be sold to His murderers for a trifling sum, so that even this should be full of poverty and dishonour for Him! By being bought He willed to share the lot of a slave and be subject to outrageous treatment. He considered it gain to be dishonoured for our sake; by being sold for a trifling sum He would hint that He came freely, as a Gift, to suffer death for the world. Willingly He died, having wronged no one either for the sake of His own life or for the common good, supplying graces to His murderers far greater than they could wish or hope for.

But why do I mention these things? It is God who died; it was God's blood which was shed upon the cross.* What could be more precious than this death, what more awesome? How great a sin had human nature committed that needed so great a penalty to expiate it! How great was the wound that required the power of this remedy!

It was necessary that sin should be abolished by some penalty, and that we, by paying a just penalty, should be cleared of the indictment of the sins which we have committed against God. He who has been punished for the things which he has committed will not be called to account for them

---

*That is, the humanity which underwent death belonged to the second Person of the Blessed Trinity. Cabasilas would hardly have subscribed to the heresy of Patripassianism, i.e., that the divine nature as such underwent either suffering or death!

again. But among men there was no one who, himself being guiltless, might have suffered for the others. Since no one could have sufficed for himself, even the whole race, could it have died ten thousand times, was unable to pay the penalty it deserved. What fitting penalty could that most wretched slave undergo, who had utterly destroyed the image of the king and acted contemptuously towards so great a dignity?

It is for this reason that the Master who is without sin suffers many terrible things and dies and endures the blow. As man He undertakes the cause of mankind. He releases our race from the indictment and gives freedom to the prisoners, since He Himself, being God and Master, stood in no need thereof.

[§ 11. The Mysteries as the means by which
     we appropriate Christ's saving work]

These, then, are the reasons why the true life passes to us through the Saviour's death. This is the way in which we draw this life into our souls—by being initiated into the Mysteries, being washed and anointed and partaking of the holy table. When we do these things, Christ comes to us and dwells in us, He is united to us and grows into one with us. He stifles sin in us and infuses into us His own life and merit and makes us to share in His victory. O how great is His goodness! He crowns those who have been washed, and those who partake of His banquet He proclaims victors.

How shall we explain that victory and its crown, the fruit of toil and sweat, which come from the baptismal washing, the chrismation, and the banquet? For though we neither struggle nor suffer when we celebrate these rites, we yet sing the praise of that struggle and celebrate that victory and venerate the trophy and display fervent and unutterable love for that Champion. As for those wounds and bruises and that death, we make them our own and apply them to ourselves by whatever means we may, and become one flesh with Him—with Him who was put to death and rose again. Wherefore we fittingly enjoy the benefits which come from that death and those struggles.

Suppose some one passing by should try to rescue a captured tyrant awaiting his punishment, in order to crown him and honour his tyranny. At his fall would he not consider himself to die and cry out against the laws and protest against justice, all this without shame or hiding his wickedness, but boldly and brazenly testifying and making a display? What verdict would we think fit for him? Would we not punish him like the tyrant? Obviously, in every way!

On the other hand, let us suppose the completely opposite case—one who admires the victor and rejoices when he has won and weaves for him the victor's crowns, rouses applause in the crowd and moves the audience, with pleasure pays him homage to his triumph, kisses his face, grasps his right hand, and is thus utterly beside himself over the hero and the victory which he has won, as though it were he whose head was to be crowned. In the eyes of favourable judges this man would have some share in the victor's prizes, just as the other would share in the tyrant's punishment. If in the case of the wicked the just penalty must be exacted and their purpose and intent must be taken into account, it would hardly be right that the good should be deprived of their deserts. In addition, were the victor himself to stand in no need of the prizes of his victory but prefer above all to see his admirer to enjoy the honour of the audience and regard the crowning of his friend as his own prize in the contest— would it not be most fitting, most appropriate, that the latter should carry off the crown, even though without the sweat and peril of the conflict?

These things, then, this baptismal washing and the banquet and the sober enjoyment of the chrism achieve. For when we are initiated we despise the tyrant, we spit at him and we shun him; as for our Champion we praise Him, we admire Him, we worship Him and love Him with all our soul, so that we by overflowing love feed on Him as on bread, we are anointed with Him as by chrism, we are clothed with Him as by water. It is evident that He undertook the warfare on our behalf and that for the sake of our victory He endured death. Thus there is nothing unfitting or incongruous that we should attain to the crowns of victory through these Mysteries. On our part we display such eagerness as we are able, when we hear that this water has the power of Christ's death and tomb; we believe it most firmly and gladly draw near and go down into the water.

They are no trifling gifts that He bestows, nor are they trifling benefits of which He counts us worthy! Those who come over to Him He welcomes with the gifts which follow from His death and burial. He does not merely bestow a crown or give them some share in His glory, He gives them Himself, the Victor who is crowned with glory. When we come up from the water we bear the Saviour upon our souls, on our heads, on our eyes, in our very inward parts, on all our members—Him who is pure from sin, free from all corruption, just as He was when He rose again and appeared to His disciples, as He was taken up, as He will come again to demand the return of His treasure.

Thus we have been born; we have been stamped with Christ as though with some figure and shape. To prevent us from introducing any alien figure He Himself occupies the entrances of life. He appropriates the organs by which we introduce air and food to aid the life of the body, and through them He enters our souls; through the former He comes as chrism and a sweet odour, through the latter as food. We breathe Him, He becomes food for us. Thus, as He blends and mingles Himself with us throughout, He makes us His own body and He becomes for us what a head is for the members of a body. Since, then, He is the Head, we share all good things with Him, for that which belongs to the head must needs pass into the body.

For this reason one might well marvel that we do not share in His stripes and death also, but that, while He alone underwent that struggle, yet when He was to be crowned He then made us partakers of Himself. This too belongs to His ineffable loving-kindness. Yet it is not without reason or contrary to it. It was after the cross that we were united to Christ; before He had died we had nothing in common with Him. He was the Son and the beloved One, but we were unclean, slaves, of a hostile mind. It was when He had died and the ransom had been paid and the devil's prison had been destroyed that we obtained freedom and adoption of sons and became members of that blessed Head. From Him, therefore, that which belongs to the Head becomes ours as well.

Now, then, we depart from this water without sin. Because of the chrism we partake of His graces, and because of the banquet we live with the same life He does. In the world to come we shall be gods with God,* fellow-heirs with Him of the same riches, reigning with Him in the same kingdom—that is, unless we of our own free will blind ourselves in this life and rend asunder the royal garment. This alone we contribute to this life—that we submit to His gifts, retain His graces, and do not reject the crown which God by many toils and labours has prepared for us.

This is the life in Christ which the Mysteries confer, but to which, apparently, human effort also has a contribution to make. He, then, who would speak thereof must first deal with each of the Mysteries. After that it is fitting to consider the activity which is in accordance with virtue.

---

*"He was made man that we might be made God"—St. Athanasius, *On the Incarnation*, 54. The Orthodox Church lays great stress on the Christian life as deification, or divinization—not, indeed, that we might be absorbed into the divine essence, but be penetrated by the divine "energies." See further: V. Lossky, *The Mystical Theology of the Eastern Church*, Chapter 5.

THE SECOND BOOK

*What contribution Holy Baptism makes to
the life in Christ*

[§ 1. How the Holy Mysteries
unite us to Christ]

In the foregoing it has been shown that the holy life is
brought about by the sacred Mysteries. Let us now examine
how each of the Mysteries leads to this life. Since the life
in Christ means to be united with Christ, let us now explain
how each sacred rite unites to Christ those who have
undergone it.

Union with Christ, then, belongs to those who have
undergone all that the Saviour has undergone, and have
experienced and become all that He has. Now He was
united to blood and flesh pure from all sin. By nature
He Himself is God from the very beginning, and that
which He afterwards assumed, human nature, He has
deified. Finally He died for the sake of the flesh, and
rose again.

He who seeks to be united with Him must therefore
share with Him in His flesh, partake of deification, and
share in His death and resurrection. So we are baptized
in order that we may die that death and rise again in that

resurrection. We are chrismated in order that we may
become partakers of the royal anointing of His deification.
By feeding on the most sacred bread and drinking the most
divine cup we share in the very Flesh and Blood which the
Saviour assumed.

In this way we are joined to Him who for our sake
was incarnate and who deified our nature, who died and
rose again. Why then do we not observe the same order
as He, but begin where He left off and reach the end
where He began? It is because He descended in order that
we might ascend. It is by the same path that it was His
task to descend, that it is ours to ascend. As in the case of
a ladder, that which was His last step as He descended is
for us the first step as we ascend. It could not be otherwise
because of the very nature of things.

Baptism, then, is birth. The chrism conveys the principle
of energy and movement; the bread of life and the cup
of thanksgiving are true food and drink (cf. Jn. 6:55).
Before being born it is impossible to be moved or fed.
Further, Baptism reconciles man to God, the chrism makes
him worthy of the gifts from on high; the power of the
table communicates the Flesh and Blood of Christ to him
who is initiated. It is impossible, before one has been
reconciled, to stand among God's friends or to be counted
worthy of the graces that befit them. Those who are subject
to the evil one and to sins cannot drink the Blood and eat
the Flesh which belong to the sinless one. Accordingly, we
are first washed, then anointed, and thus the banquet receives
us in a state of purity and with a sweet odour.

Let this then suffice. Now let us examine what advantage
each of the Mysteries brings to the holy life, and first of
all what great things Baptism can contribute to this life.

[§ 2.   **Baptism as the new birth in Christ**]

To be baptized, then, is to be born according to Christ
and to receive our very being and nature, having previously
been nothing. This we can learn from many sources. First,

from the very order itself: it is the first of the Mysteries into which we are initiated, and before the others this Mystery introduces Christians into the new life. Secondly, we may learn this from the very names which we call it, and thirdly, from the ceremonies which we employ and the words which we sing.

This, then, is the order which we follow. First we are washed, then, when we have been anointed with chrism, we approach the sacred table. This is a clear proof that the baptismal washing is the beginning of life, its foundation and presupposition, that Christ Himself, who endured all things for our sake, considered it necessary to be baptized and underwent this before all else. As for the names, what else could they imply? We call it "birth," "new birth," "new creation," and "seal," and in addition "baptism" [i.e., "dipping"], "clothing," "anointing," "charisma" [i.e., "gift"], "illumination," and "washing." These all signify this one thing, that this rite is the beginning of being for those who are in accordance with God and so live.

Properly, then, "birth" appears to signify nothing else than this. "New birth" and "new creation" mean nothing else than that those who are born and created have been born previously and have lost their original form, but now return to it by a second birth. It is as when the material of a statue has lost its shape and a sculptor restores and refashions the image, since it is a form and shape effected in us by Baptism. It engraves an image and imparts a form to our souls by conforming them to the death and resurrection of the Saviour. It is thus also called a "seal," since it conforms us to the image of the King and to His blessed form. Since the form clothes the material and puts an end to its formlessness we also call the Mystery "clothing" and "baptism" [dipping"].

This is what Paul declares when he applies to it the terms "clothing" and "seal." At one time he speaks of Christ being engraved and formed on Christians, at other times as being wrapped around them like a garment. He speaks of the initiate as having been clothed and plunged into water, writing to the Galatians, "my little children, with

whom I am again in travail until Christ be formed in you"
(4:19), and "Jesus Christ was portrayed in you as crucified"
(cf. 3:1), and "as many of you as were baptized into Christ
have put on Christ" (3:27, cf. 1 Cor. 15:53, 2 Cor. 5:3).
For until gold, silver, and bronze are softened and melted
by fire, they are mere materials to the onlooker, so that
they are called merely by the name of the material, "gold"
or "silver" or "bronze." But when each acquires a shape from
the blows of the iron tools it is no longer the material only,
but the shape which appears to the onlookers, just as
clothes become apparent to them before the bodies which
they cover. Accordingly each receives a proper appellation,
such as "statue," "ring," or something else which no longer
indicates the material but the appearance or form only.

Perhaps this is why the saving day of Baptism becomes
the name's day for Christians. It is then that we are formed
and shaped, and our shapeless and undefined life receives
shape and definition. Besides, we become known to Him
who knows His own, as Paul says, "having come to know
God, or rather, to be known by God" (Gal. 4:9). On this
day we hear the significant word, our name, as though then
we were properly known, for to be known by God is to
become truly known. For this reason David said of those
who have no part in this life, "I will not make mention
of their names upon my lips" (Ps. 16:4), since those who
have removed themselves far from this light are unknown
and unseen. Apart from light nothing is visible to the eyes
of those who can see, nor is he known to God who has
not received light from above. This is the reason: unless
it becomes apparent to Him by the light it entirely lacks
true existence. This is in accordance with the saying, "The
Lord knows those who are His" (2 Tim. 2:19, Num. 16:5).
Again of the foolish virgins He says that He knows them
not (Mt. 25:12).

For this reason Baptism is called "illumination." Since
it confers true being it makes men known to God; because
it leads to that light it removes from darkness and
wickedness. Because it is an illumination it is also called a
"washing." Since it removes all defilement it bestows on men

pure converse with the light, removing as it were a barrier which blocks off the divine radiance from our souls.

Baptism is called "gift" because it is a birth, for what might a person contribute to his own birth? As in the case of physical birth we do not contribute even the desire for all the blessings derived from Baptism, were one to examine it closely. We wish for the things which we are able to conceive in our minds, but these blessings "the heart of man has not conceived" (1 Cor. 2:9), and no one could imagine them before experiencing them. When we hear of the possibility of freedom and kingship we think in terms of a happy life which human thoughts can grasp. But this is entirely different, greater than both our thought and our desire.

Baptism is called "anointing" because on those who are initiated it engraves Christ, who was anointed for us. It is a "seal" wrich imprints the Saviour Himself. As the anointing is actually applied to the whole form of the body of him who is anointed, so it imprints on him the Anointed One and displays His form and is really a sealing.

By what has been said it has been shown that the seal has the same effect as the birth, just as the clothing and the plunging effect the same as the sealing. Since the free gift, the illumination, and the washing have the same effect as the new creation and the birth, it is evident that all the nomenclature of Baptism signifies one thing—the baptismal washing is our birth and the beginning of our life in Christ. But whether the ceremonies and words of the Mystery express this meaning will be clear to us as we go over the rite in detail.

[§ 3.   How the various ceremonies preceding Baptism prepare for the new life in Christ]

(a) The exorcism

It is apparent, then, that before he has been initiated he who approaches the Mystery has not yet been reconciled to God and has not yet been set free from the primeval disgrace. As the candidate draws near, the officiant, before he performs any other ceremony, prays that he may be released from the demon who possesses him. He not only addresses God on the candidate's behalf, but attacks the very tyrant himself by rebuking him and driving him out by scourging. As for his scourge, it is "the name which is above every name" (Phil. 2:9).

(b) The insufflation

So far is the catechumen from life and from being a son and an heir, that he is still enslaved to the tyrant, since he who is united to the evil one is totally separated from God, which means that he is completely dead. Therefore, since he has not yet received a share in life, the celebrant breathes into his face, for the inbreathing from above is a symbol of life.

(c) The stripping of the candidate

The things which follow correspond to each other, for they all pertain to the decision made by rejecting the things which are here and now and changing over to other things. The candidate is urged to despise one world and to honour the other, to rid himself of one life and with all eagerness to pursue the other. Accordingly, by the acts by which he lays aside things present it is evident that he is not yet freed from the things which he has condemned. By the acts by which he accepts from this Mystery those things which he thinks better and preferable to things present, he shows that he begins the life which he approves of, by being baptized.

As he enters the sacred house he lays aside his garment and takes off his shoes, thus symbolizing his former life by these aids to living, the garment and the shoes.

(d) The renunciation

Further, as he turns towards the west he breathes from his mouth, which is a sign of the life which is in darkness. He stretches forth his hands and repels the evil one as though he were present and pressing upon him. Those most hateful covenants of unbelief which are the cause of all ruin he disowns and completely breaks off that bitter friendship, and praises enmity [with the evil one].

(e) The recitation of the Nicene Creed

Fleeing from darkness he runs towards the light and turns to the east to seek the sun. Being freed from the tyrant's hands he worships the King, and having condemned the usurper he recognizes his lawful Master. He prays that he may become subject to Him and serve Him with all his soul, and above all that he may believe in Him as God and know the things which pertain to Him.* For it is the true knowledge of God which is the beginning of the blessed life, since as Solomon says, "to know Thee is the root of immortality" (Wis. 15:3), just as it was ignorance of God which brought in death at the beginning. Since Adam did not know the divine loving-kindness, he thought that the Good One was envious, and forgetting wisdom he thought that he was hidden from the Wise One; so he adhered to the runaway slave and despised his Master. For this reason he was expelled from Paradise and deprived of life and suffered pain and died. The knowledge of God, then, must come first for him who hastens towards life and towards God.

As we are entirely stripped and lay aside the last garment we now show that we lay hold on the way that leads to Paradise and on the life that is there. For, when Adam fell into nakedness out of that robe of happiness, he came

---

*Note the question and answer immediately preceding the Creed: "Dost thou believe in Him?" "I believe in Him as King and as God."

from it into this wretched garb. But as we proceed from "the garments of skin" (Gen. 3:21) and undergo being stripped we clearly show that we return by the same way and hasten to the royal garment. We return to the same place and by the same way that He descended into this world. Let then the stripping be the sign of that as well, that we now approach in purity to the true Light, taking nothing with us. So the shadow of death and whatever else blocks off the blessed light from the souls of men are like the garments, a wall between the light and our bodies.

(f) The anointing before Baptism

To understand what the anointing with oil may signify, let us consider Jacob's pillar which he offered to God by anointing it with oil, and the kings and priests who are consecrated to the community and to God in this very way. In no way do they live for themselves, but for God and the commonwealth for which they have been appointed. We ourselves have also withdrawn from our own life and from ourselves to God. This means that we cast off our old form and become like Him. So the symbol is proper and very fitting for our appellation of "Christians," for we are anointed, and He whom we aim to resemble is Christ who has anointed human nature with divinity, since we share with Him in His anointing also. Thus our anointing is the sign of His anointing, which the celebrant indicates by reciting over him who is being initiated and anointed the very words by which David refers to the anointing and kingship of Christ. As he names him who is being initiated the priest says, "(This person) is anointed with the oil of gladness." When David refers to the Saviour he says, "God, even thy God, hath anointed thee with the oil of gladness above thy fellows" (Ps. 45:7). By "fellows" He means us, whom God of His loving-kindness makes partakers of the kingdom.

[§ 4. The baptismal act and its significance]

Until these things we do not yet live. These ceremonies are signs to him that is being initiated, preliminaries and preparations for life. But as soon as he has thrice emerged from the water after being submerged* therein during the invocation of the Trinity, he who has been initiated receives all that he seeks. He is born and receives form by that birth which is of the day which David mentions (Ps. 139:16 LXX). He receives the noble seal and possesses all the happiness which he has sought. He who once was darkness becomes light; he who once was nothing now has existence. He enters God's household and is like a son who has been adopted; from the dungeon and utmost slavery he is led to the royal throne.

So this water destroys the one life and brings the other into the open; it drowns the old man and raises up the new. This becomes clear from the very acts themselves for those who have experienced them; afterwards the very things which are visible in the Mystery make it possible in every way to infer this. In that he vanishes by sinking into the water he appears to flee from the life which is in the air. To flee from life is to die; but by again emerging and returning to the air and the light he appears to seek and obtain life.

For this cause we here invoke the Creator, since what takes place here is a beginning of life and a second creation which is far better than the first. The image [of God in man] is delineated more accurately than before, and the statue is molded more clearly according to the divine pattern; wherefore the archetype must needs be the more perfectly set forth.

[§ 5. The invocation of the Threefold Name]

When those who perform Baptism invoke God over the

---

*In the Orthodox Church Baptism is normally by immersion, rarely by affusion, never by sprinkling.

act of washing it is not by the common name "God" that they call the Trinity. It would not suffice for those who theologize clearly and distinctly; but rather they proclaim the proper nature of each of the Persons with more precision and exactitude.

There is this reason as well. Even though it is by one single act of loving-kindness that the Trinity has saved our race, yet each of the blessed Persons is said to have contributed something of His own. It is the Father who is reconciled, the Son who reconciles, while the Holy Spirit is bestowed as a gift on those who have become friends. The Father has set us free, the Son was the ransom by which we were freed, but the Spirit is freedom, for Paul says, "where the Spirit of the Lord is, there is freedom" (2 Cor. 3:17). The Father has re-shaped us, by means of the Son we were re-shaped, but "it is the Spirit who gives life" (Jn. 6:63). The Trinity was foreshadowed even at the first creation. Then the Father created, and the Son was the hand for Him who created,* but the Paraclete was the breath for Him who inbreathed the life.

Why say I these things? It is only in God's act of saving man that His distinctions appear. While there are many benefits which God in every age has bestowed upon creation, yet you will find none which is referred solely to the Father, or to the Son, or to the Holy Spirit, but all are common to the Trinity, because He performs all things by one power and one providence and one creation. But in the dispensation by which He restored our race this novel thing took place. It is the Trinity who jointly willed my salvation and provided how it would take place, yet no longer jointly effects it, for neither the Father nor the Spirit, but the Logos alone Himself achieves it. It was the Only-begotten alone who took on Himself flesh and blood and suffered wounds, torments, and death, and who rose again. Through these things our nature revived and Baptism, the new birth and new creation, came into being.

---

*Note the statements of the Nicene Creed: "through whom all things were made" (concerning the Son), and "the Giver of life" (concerning the Holy Spirit).

It was needful, therefore, for those who call upon God over the divine washing to distinguish between the Persons by calling on the Father, the Son, and the Holy Spirit, as they provide the sacred re-creation which alone shows forth God as thus distinguished.

[§ 6. How we in Baptism appropriate the saving acts of Christ]

What then? Do we not also at Baptism celebrate the divine dispensation, and it above all? Indeed so, not so much by what we say, but by our actions. Who does not know that the threefold immersion and emersion represent the three days' death of the Saviour and His resurrection, the climax of the whole dispensation? It is not, I think, without reason that we proclaim aloud the doctrine of God, but display the dispensation by silent actions. The former was in the beginning and came to the knowledge of men by the voice alone, the latter happened subsequently and was seen by the eyes of men and was touched and handled. Accordingly the blessed John who knew both the former and the latter alike, relating to the Saviour in His duality, declared both "that which was from the beginning, which we have heard," and that "which we have seen with our eyes, which our hands have touched, concerning the Word of life" (1 Jn. 1:1).

Further, it is necessary only to believe in the doctrine, and the demonstration of the faith consists in the utterance, for, as Paul says, "man believes with his heart and so is justified, and he confesses with his lips, and so is saved" (Rom. 10:10). As for the dispensation, it is altogether necessary that it be imitated and shown forth in our deeds, for, as Peter says, we must "follow in His steps" (1 Pet. 2:21) the One who died for us and rose again.

For these reasons, then, the Trinity is named in words, but the passion and the bodily death we represent by means of the water, and conform ourselves to that blessed image and form. From what has been said it is thus evident that from all the visible acts in Baptism, from the very order itself, the names which we call it, the ceremonies which are performed in it, and the words which accompany it, we learn that the life in Christ receives the beginning of its existence from the baptismal washing.

[§ 7.   Baptism and original sin]

But it remains to be examined what the very essence of this life is. Since we destroy something and become something else, and discard something while preserving another, if it becomes clear what either of these is, it may become clear what it means to be in accordance with Christ. Now the former is sin, the latter is righteousness. The one is the old man, the other is the new. Let us then look more closely into these matters.

Sin is twofold: it extends into the areas both of action and habit. The action does not linger for a time, nor does it remain at all. It happens once and is no more, like an arrow which is shot and passes by; yet it leaves a wound in those who commit it, the traces of wickedness, the disgrace and the liability to punishment.

The habit of sin arises from evil actions, like a disease introduced by tainted food. It is permanent and chains souls with unbreakable fetters. It enslaves the mind and brings about the worst effects of all by inciting its captives to commit the most wicked actions. It is produced by them and constantly engenders them; it is born and similarly gives birth in a vicious circle. Accordingly sin has no end, since the habit gives rise to the actions and the accumulation of actions aggravates the habit. Thus the evils are mutually reinforced and constantly progress, so that "sin came to life, but I died" (Rom. 7:9).

It was neither yesterday nor the day before that the evil began, but at the time that we began to exist. As soon as Adam despised his good Master by believing the evil one and was perverted in will, his soul lost its health and well-being. From that time on his body agreed with the soul and was in accord with it, and was perverted with it like an instrument in the hand of the craftsman. The soul shares its passions with the body by being closely united to it, as is shown by the fact that the body blushes when the soul is ashamed and wastes away when the soul is beset with anxieties. Because our nature was extended and our race increased as it proceeded from the first body, so wickedness too, like any other natural characteristic, was transmitted to the bodies which proceeded from that body.

The body, then, not merely shares in the experiences of the soul but also imparts its own experiences to the soul. The soul is subject to joy or vexation, is restrained or unrestrained, depending on the disposition of the body. It therefore followed that each man's soul inherited the wickedness of the first Adam. It spread from his soul to his body, and from his body to the bodies which derived from his, and from those bodies to the souls.

This, then, is the old man whom we have received as a seed of evil from our ancestors as we came into existence. We have not seen even one day pure from sin, nor have we ever breathed apart from wickedness, but, as the psalmist says, "we have gone astray from the womb, we err from our birth" (Ps. 58:4). We did not even stand still in this unhappy lot of the sin of our ancestors, nor were we content with the evils which we had inherited. So greatly have we added to the wickedness and increased the abundance of evil that the primal sin has been covered over by that which came later and the imitators have shown themselves to be worse by far than the examples.

Worst of all, there was no intermission of the evil, but the disease progressed continually. Perhaps it was for this reason that it was impossible for the human race to suffice for curing itself. Since it had scarcely ever tasted of freedom or had any experience of it, it was unable even to attain to a longing for it or a wish to obtain it and to revolt against tyranny.

It is from these most terrible bonds, this punishment, disease, and death, that the baptismal washing sets us free. This it does so easily that there is no need to take a

long time, so perfectly that not a trace is left. Nor
does it merely set us free from wickedness, it also confers
the opposite condition. Because of His death the Master
Himself gave us the power to slay sin, and because He
came to life again He made us heirs of the new life. His
death, by being a death slays the evil life, by being a
penalty it pays the penalty for sins to which each one of us
was liable for our evil actions.

In this way the baptismal washing renders us pure of
every habit and action of sin in that it makes us partakers
of Christ's life-giving health.

[§ 8.   The deliverance which Baptism obtains for us]

Since we share in His resurrection through the baptismal
washing Christ gives us another life, and forms members
and provides the faculties needed by those who attain to the
life to come. It is for this reason that I am completely
released from the indictments and forthwith receive health,
particularly because it is entirely the work of God who
cannot be subject to time.

Further, it is not merely at this present time that He
benefits our race, as though He needed time, but He has
already done so. It is not now that the Master is paying the
penalty for the sins which I have committed, or preparing
the cure and forming the members and providing the
faculties, but He has already done so. It was when He
mounted the cross and died and rose again that the freedom
of mankind came about, that the form and the beauty were
created and the new members were prepared. All, then, that
is needed now is to approach and draw near to the gifts.

This is what the baptismal washing accomplishes for
us. It brings the dead to life, the captives to freedom, the
mutilated it provides with the blessed form. The ransom
has already been paid; now we are merely being released.
The chrism has been poured forth and its sweet odour
encompasses everything; all that remains is to breathe it.

Or rather, not even the breathing remains for us, since the ability to breathe it has been prepared by the Saviour, as well as the possibility of being released and enlightened. By coming into the world He not merely rose as its Light, but even provided the eye to see it. He not merely poured forth the chrism but even gave the means of perceiving it. This sacred washing joins our organs and faculties to those who have been washed. Like formless and shapeless matter we go down into this water; in it we meet with the form that is beautiful.

That is why all blessings arise for us at the same time. They were prepared for us beforehand, as is said, "Behold, I have made ready my dinner, my oxen and my fat calves are killed, and everything is ready; come to the marriage feast" (Mt. 22:4). This alone is lacking at the feast—that those who have been invited should come.

In the case of those who come, what more is needed for happiness? Nothing whatever. In the world to come we shall come to Christ duly prepared, but now, having approached Him, we are being prepared. At that time we must have all things in order so that we may approach Him, but now those who approach must receive all things. It is for this reason that the foolish virgins will not then be able to come to the bridal chamber, while in the present age He calls the unwise to the feasting and the toasts of friendship. Then it will be impossible for the dead to revive, for the blind to see, and the deformed to be formed anew. In this present life only the will and the eagerness are needed and all things follow, for He says, "I came into the world that they might have life" (Jn. 10:10), and "I have come as light into the world" (Jn. 12:46).

It is of His ineffable loving-kindness that He has accomplished all things by which we have been released. He left something for us to contribute to our freedom—that we should believe that by Baptism we have salvation and that we should willingly approach it, so that from thence everything should be imputed to us, and that gratitude should be due for the things by which He has benefited us. Whenever, then, it happens that those who have been

washed straightway depart this life and bring with them
nothing but the seal of Baptism, He calls them to their
crowns as though they had striven for the kingdom.

[§ 9.   How Baptism confers newness of life in Christ]

From these things, and in this manner Baptism sets
free our souls. But since it confers life, life on account of
Him who has risen again, let us inquire what that life is.
It is reasonable indeed that it should not be the same as
that by which we have lived in the past, but one far excelling
the former, and with a nature of its own. Were it the former
life which we have now, why did we have to die? Were
it another having the same power, this would be no
resurrection. Were it an angelic one, what have we in common
with the angels? It is man who has fallen, but if an angel
had risen when man had fallen man would not have been
created anew. It would have been as though, when a statue
had been shattered, it were not the form of a man but
some other likeness which was imposed on the bronze, for
this would be forming something else instead of refashioning
the statue.

For this reason it follows that this life is both a human
life and a new one superior to the former. It is by the
Saviour's life alone that all these things take place: It is
a new life because it has nothing to do with the old life,
it is inconceivably superior since it belongs to God. It has
a nature of its own, for it was the life of a man. As He
who lived it was man just as He is God, so He was pure
from all sin for the sake of human nature. For these reasons
it is altogether necessary that the life of Christ should rise
as a sun for us as we are born anew, and this is why we
depart from this water without sin.

By this also it will be clear. The birth in Baptism is
the beginning of the life to come, and the provision of new
members and faculties is the preparation for that manner
of life. But it is impossible to be prepared for the future

life unless we receive the life of Christ here and now. He became "the Father of the age to come" (Is. 9:5 LXX) just as Adam became the father of the present age, for it was Adam himself who inaugurated for mankind the life which lies in corruption. Just as it is impossible to live this natural life without receiving the organs of Adam and the human facultes necessary for this life, so likewise no one can attain that blessed world alive without being prepared by the life of Christ and being formed according to His image.

In yet another way the baptismal washing is a birth. It is Christ who bestows birth and we who are born; and as for him who is being born, it is quite clear that He who generates confers His own life on him.

[§ 10.   Excursus—on the resurrection of the dead]

At this too one might well be astounded: that it is not only those who have been baptized, but even those for whom it was impossible to be prepared for life immortal by the power of the Mysteries—in short, it is all men who will receive ageless bodies and rise incorruptible. It is indeed amazing that they should share in the resurrection which Christ's death alone brought into the world, who have not received the baptismal washing whereby we share in His life-giving death. If they have fled from the Physician and refused His aid and shunned the only remedy, what else would there be which would suffice them for immortality? It would seem reasonable that one or the other should happen: either that all men henceforth should enjoy the benefits of which Christ by His death is the Author, and rise with Him and live with Him and reign with Him and have all that belongs to blessedness, since "He has no need of our good" (Ps. 16:2) ; or else, since it is entirely necessary that we contribute something, that those who have not contributed faith should not live again with the Saviour.

To this we must reply as follows. The resurrection is the restoration of our human nature. Such things God gives

freely, for just as He forms us without us willing it, so
He forms us anew though we have contributed nothing to
it. On the other hand, the kingdom and vision of God
and union with Christ are privileges which depend on
willingness. They are thus possible only for those who have
been willing to receive them and have loved them and longed
for them. For such it is fitting to enjoy the presence of the
things for which they longed; for the unwilling it is
impossible. How can one be capable of enjoying and finding
delight in the presence of things for which one had no
longing when they were absent? One would not be able
to desire them then and seek to obtain them since one could
not see that beauty and, as the Lord says, "he cannot receive
it, because he does not see it, nor does he know it" (Jn.
14:17). Like a blind man he would fall out of this life
into that, bereft of every sense and faculty by which it is
possible to know and love the Saviour and to wish to be
united to Him and be able to achieve it.

One need not therefore marvel that while all will live
in immortality, it is not all who will live in blessedness.
All equally enjoy God's providence for our nature, but it
is only those who are devout towards God who enjoy the
gifts which adorn their willingness. This is the reason: God
indeed wills all good things for all men and imparts to all
alike of all His own gifts, both those which benefit the
will and those which restore nature. On our part we all
receive the gifts of God which pertain to nature even though
we do not desire them, since we cannot escape them. So
He does good to those who are unwilling and compels them
lovingly. Whenever we wish to shake off His kindness we
are unable to do so.

Such is the gift of the resurrection. It is not within our
power either to be born or to return to life after we have
died, nor to do the opposite. As for the things which depend
on human willingness, such as choosing that which is good,
the forgiveness of sins, uprightness of character, purity of
soul, love of God—their reward is final blessedness. These
things we have the power to accept or to shun. Therefore
those who are willing are able to enjoy them, but as for

the unwilling, how would it be possible? It is impossible for the unwilling to wish for them, or to be compelled to be willing.

It is the Lord alone who released human nature from corruption, since He on the one hand became "the first-born from the dead" (Col. 1:18) and, on the other hand, entered for us as a forerunner into the Holy of Holies (Heb. 6:20). He has slain sin and reconciled us to God and destroyed the dividing wall (Eph. 2:14) and consecrated Himself for us (Jn. 17:19), in order that we too might be justly freed from corruption and from sin who have both will and nature in common with Him. The nature we have in common with Him by being men, and the will by loving His appearing and His passion (cf. 2 Tim. 4:8), and by being obedient to His commandments and willing what He wills.

Some there are who fulfil the one condition, but not at all the other. On the one hand they are human, on the other hand they do not entrust their salvation to the Saviour and are not at one with Him in goodness of will. It follows, then, that they fall short of the forgiveness of sins and the crown of righteousness because they are at variance with Him in will; yet since they have the same nature as Christ nothing hinders them from being set free [i.e., from death] and rising again. It is not of life as such, but only of the blessed life in Christ that Baptism is the cause. In a word, it is the fact that Christ died and came to life again which has bestowed immortal life on all alike.

For this reason the resurrection is the gift common to all men, but remission of sins, the heavenly crowns, and the kingdom become theirs alone who have given due cooperation, who have so ordered themselves in this life as to be familiar with that life and with the Bridegroom. They have been born anew since He is the new Adam, they are resplendent with beauty and have preserved the youth which the baptismal washing infused into them, for He is "fairer than the children of men" (Ps. 45:2). They stand with heads uplifted like the Olympic victors because He is their crown; they give ear because He is the Word; they lift up their eyes because He is a sun; they breathe deeply because the Bridegroom is a sweet odour and ointment poured forth (Cant. 1:3),* they are stately even in vesture because of the wedding feast.

[§ 11.   How apostasy cannot destroy
Christ's gift]

Granted these things, they lead to another problem which cannot be overlooked. It is the act of willing and believing and drawing near which results in attaining to the gifts of Baptism. To flee from these things is to flee from all that blessedness. What of those who have cast away the gifts after they have received them, and have blamed themselves for their former purpose and have denied Christ, yet afterwards, being moved by repentance, return to the Church after acting lawlessly? It would be fitting were the sacred ordinance to lead them back to the baptismal washing and repeat the mystic rites from the beginning, as though they had lost all. Yet it merely signs their bodies with the divine chrism and adds no more, and enrolls them in the circle of the faithful.**

What should one say to these things? By two things we are enabled to be devoted to God: the receiving of the eye from the Mysteries, and the use thereof for looking towards the [divine] ray of light. Do then those who betray Christianity lose the latter while retaining the former, that is, the ability and aptitude for seeing? The reason why it is so is that it is possible for those who so desire to reject [the use of the former]. It is in our power either to love the sun or to shut the eye to its ray. It is, however, impossible for us to gouge out that eye itself and entirely destroy its form. For if we are by no means able to destroy any of the faculties of the soul which are naturally inborn in us, least of all are we able to destroy that which God placed

---

*A reference to the holy chrism.

**The Orthodox Church receives repentant apostates (to Islam or other non-Christian religions) by chrismation.

in us Himself when He regenerated us. The baptismal
washing forms and disposes the leading principle in us,
whether we consider it to be autonomy of reason and will,
or anything else. To it every faculty of the soul gives away
and depends on its impulse. But it is subject to no control
or change, not even from itself, for nothing can get the
better of itself. Nor is it reasonable that even God should
change it, for He would not deprive us of any of the gifts
which He has bestowed upon us, for it says, "the gifts of
God are irrevocable" (Rom. 11:29). In short, since He is
infinite in goodness He wills for us every good thing and
bestows it on us, subject to the free exercise of our own
will.

Such, then, is the benefit of Baptism. It does not throttle
or restrain the will. Since it is a faculty nothing prevents
those who enjoy its use from living in wickedness if they so
wish, just as the possession of a sound eye would not prevent
those who desire it from living in darkness. There is further
proof of this—the evident witness of those who after
receiving Baptism and all its gifts have been carried away
to the extremes of impiety and wickedness. Therefore, since
they have not lost the infused faculties and do not need a
second forming, the priest by no means baptizes them afresh.
But by chrismating them he imparts to them the spiritual
grace of godliness, that is, fear of God, love, and the like,
which avail to renew them in their former purpose, for it
is such things that the chrism is able to do for those who
are initiated.

Let this be enough of those matters, and let us proceed
with the rest of the discussion.

[§ 12.   Baptism and the powers of
the age to come]

From what has been said it is clear that those who have
been born through Baptism live the life of Christ. But what
is the life of Christ? I mean, what is that condition which
those who have benefited by Baptism and have been washed

therein have in common with Christ in their life? This has
not yet been made clear; indeed, the greater part of it
surpasses human reason. It is the power of the world to
come, as Paul says (Heb. 6:5), and a preparation for another
life. Just as it is impossible to understand what the eyes
can do or the beauty of colour without coming to the light,
or for sleepers while they are still asleep to learn of the
actions of those who stay awake, so it is impossible in this
life to know clearly the new members and their faculties
and how great is their beauty, since it is only in the life
to come that they can be used. For this there is need of
a similar beauty and a corresponding light.

Yet we are really members of Christ, and this is the
result of Baptism. The splendor and beauty of the members
come from the Head, for they would not appear beautiful
without being attached to the Head. The Head of these
members is hidden in the present life but He will appear
in the life to come. Then the members too will be resplendent
and will be clearly manifested when they shine brightly
with their Head. To this Paul refers when he says, "you
have died, and your life is hid with Christ in God; but
when Christ who is our life appears, then you also will
appear with Him in glory" (Col. 3:3-4). And blessed John
says, "it does not yet appear what we shall be, but when
He appears we shall be like Him" (1 Jn. 3:2).

It is therefore impossible now fully to know the power
of this life, even, I suppose, for the saints themselves. They
admit their ignorance of the greater part of it, and that they
know it dimly in a mirror and in part (1 Cor. 13:12), and
that it is impossible to express in speech even the things
which they are able to know. While those who are pure in
heart have a perception and knowledge of them, yet it is
impossible to find words of speech suitable to the objects of
knowledge and capable of expressing the blessed experience
to those who know it not. The things which the apostle
heard when he was caught up into Paradise and the third
heaven are "words which cannot be told, which man may
not utter" (2 Cor. 12:4).

[§ 13. How the effects of Baptism are shown]

That which is known of this life, of which we may speak, and which displays its hidden qualities is the courage of the newly initiated, the new character of those who have been baptized and have persevered. Their extraordinary virtue surpasses human laws and can be ascribed neither to wisdom, nor training, nor innate ability, nor to any other human cause. Their souls have eagerly rushed into things such as man cannot readily imagine, their bodies did not quench that eagerness but endured as great pains as the soul desired. Yet soul and body have but limited power and neither the one nor the other is able to stand up under every pain. Some pains they are able to overcome, under others either the soul gives up or the body breaks down.

Nothing, however, overcame the souls and bodies of the blessed martyrs. They were able to endure and persevere against pains so great and so many that even the wildest imagination cannot conceive of them. Yet I have not mentioned that which is most novel. It was not mere endurance or perseverence on their part. It was not in the hope of surpassing rewards and a better life that they despised this present life, as though achieving such daring by some act of judgment or reasoning, like patients enduring the surgeon's cautery and scalpel. What is most novel is that they loved the very wounds and longed for the very pains, that they regarded death itself as desirable even when there was no alternative. Some of them desired sword and rack and death, and when they arrived at the testing they were the more eager. Others willingly spent their lives suffering ill-treatment and hardship without any relief and considered it their food to "die daily" (1 Cor. 15:31). Their bodies followed and assisted them as they struggled against the very laws of the body. This was true not of two or three or twenty, nor of men only or those in the prime of life, but of tens of thousands, nay rather of countless persons of every age alike.

[§ 14.   The examples of the martyrs for Christ]

Most clearly was this shown in the case of the martyrs. Some of them were believers before the persecutions; into others Christ infused the true life during the very persecutions. All alike displayed faith in Christ to their persecutors, they proclaimed the Name and were willing to die. With a single shout they challenged the executioners as though they were rushing to some obvious benefit, all of them alike, women and girls, men and boys, every occupation, every class. This too must be stated since it makes no small difference to the matter. One who lives by the sweat of hard work would not be affected in the same way by agonies and pains as one who lives a life of leisure. A soldier and a musician would not look on sword and death with the same eyes.

Yet none of these things hindered that amazing rush into martyrdom, nor did they prevent them from all alike attaining to that summit of wisdom. Since it was the one and the same power which gave birth and form to all, so they all attained to the utmost limit of virtue, and honoured and loved the good above all that is proper to nature. For His sake they despised even their very souls. Even women of the stage and degenerates and such scum received the word of our common salvation. They were changed as they were conformed to that excellent harmony, and as suddenly and easily as though they were merely changing masks.

It happened that many ended up in this choir even though they had not been washed, i.e., had not been baptized with water by the Church, yet the Church's Bridegroom Himself baptized them. To many He gave a cloud from heaven, or water sprang from the earth of its own accord, and so He baptized them. Most of them, however, He invisibly re-created. Just as the members of the Church, such as Paul and others like him, should complete what is lacking in Christ (cf. Col. 1:24), so it is not incongruous if the Head of the Church supply what is lacking in the Church. If there are some members who appear to be helping the Head, how much more fitting it is that the Head Himself should add that which is lacking for the members.

[§ 15. How Baptism enables us to endure all things for Christ]

These things being so, let us resume our subject. That this power by which they ventured with such courage and were willing to die with such zeal cannot possibly be found in human nature need not be shown by reasoning. Further, since we must suppose the grace of Baptism as its cause, let us examine the way in which the washing has effected these things in them.

Now it is clear that the labours and struggles were such as are proper to those who love, and that the darts and philtres of Christ impelled them to this novelty.* So let us examine what is the cause of their love, what they experienced to make them love in this way, and whence they received the fire of love.

In fact it is knowing that causes love and gives birth to it. It is not possible to attain love of anything that is beautiful without first learning how beautiful it is. Since this knowledge is sometimes very ample and complete and at other times imperfect, it follows that the philtre of love has a corresponding effect. Some things that are beautiful and good are perfectly known and perfectly loved as befits so great beauty. Others are not clearly evident to those who love them, and love of them is thus more feeble.

This therefore becomes clear: the baptismal washing has instilled into men some knowledge and perception of God, so that they have clearly known Him who is good and have perceived His beauty and tasted of His goodness (cf. Ps. 34:8). This, I affirm, they are able to know more perfectly by experience than were they merely to learn it by being taught.

---

*Mystical imagery which is ultimately derived, as in other spiritual writers, from the Song of Songs (Canticles) in the Old Testament.

Our knowledge of things is twofold: that which one may acquire from hearsay, and that which one may learn by personal experience. In the former we do not deal with the thing itself, but see it by means of words as in a picture, and inaccurately at that, since it is by the image of the form itself. It is impossible to find anything in nature entirely like it which would actually be an adequate copy for use by those who would acquire knowledge of it. When, however, men encounter the things themselves they gain experience of them. By experience the very form itself encounters the soul and incites desire, as though it left an imprint corresponding to the good. In the former case, since we lack the proper appearance of the thing itself, we receive an uncertain and dim image of it through that which it has in common with other things, and by it measure our desire for the thing itself. Therefore we do not love it to the extent that it is a worthy object of love, and since we have not perceived the very form itself we do not experience its proper effect. Just as a different form of anything that exists produces a different impression on the soul, so it inspires a different degree of love.

When therefore love of the Saviour produces nothing new or extraordinary in us it proves that we have encountered no more than mere words about Him. How would it be possible to know Him well from hearsay? Nothing like Him may be found, nothing which He has in common with others, nor is there anything with which He may be compared nor anything which is comparable to Him. How could one then comprehend His beauty or love Him in a way that is worthy of it?

When men have a longing so great that it surpasses human nature and eagerly desire and are able to accomplish things beyond human thought, it is the Bridegroom who has smitten them with this longing. It is He who has sent a ray of His beauty into their eyes. The greatness of the wound shows the dart which has struck home, the longing indicates who has inflicted the wound.

In this way the New Covenant differs from the Old and is superior to it. Of old it was a word which instructed;

now it is Christ Himself who is present and in an ineffable manner disposes and forms the souls of men. By means of words, teaching, and laws it was not possible for men to arrive at the goal which they sought. Had it been possible by means of words, there would have been no need for deeds, and deeds at that which were extraordinary—that God should be incarnate, be crucified, and suffer death.

[§ 16.   How experience prepared the saints]

Now this became clear at the beginning in the very fathers of our religion, the apostles. They had enjoyed all the training, and that by the Saviour Himself; they had been eyewitnesses of all things, not only of the graces which He implanted in our nature but also of the things which He underwent for mankind, how after dying He revived, and how He took possession of heaven. Yet, though they had learned all these things they exhibited nothing new, nothing noble or spiritual or superior to the old, until they had been baptized. But when they had received Baptism by the descent of the Paraclete upon their souls they not only themselves became new men and laid hold on new life, but also became leaders of others and kindled longing for Christ both in themselves and in others. Though they had been close to the Sun and shared in His daily life and discourse they had no perception of His ray until they received that spiritual washing.

In the same way as well God has perfected all the subsequent saints. They recognized and loved Him, not by being moved by mere words, but by being disposed by the power of the baptismal washing, since the Object of their love Himself disposed and formed them. He it is who "creates a pure heart" (Ps. 51:12) and "takes out the stony heart," and "gives a heart of flesh" (Ezek. 11:19, 36:26) by casting out insensitivity. He writes, as Paul says, "not on tablets of stone, but on tablets of hearts of flesh" (2 Cor. 3:5), inscribing them not merely with the Law, but with Himself, the Lawgiver.

[§ 17. How Baptism has converted
scoffers to Christ]

This has been most clearly shown by a number of the
Saints. They had been unable to learn the truth by words
and had failed to recognize the power proclaimed by
miracles; yet, once they had received the baptismal washing,
it suddenly showed them to be true Christians.

The blessed Porphyrius was born at the time when
Christ's law was prevailing in all the world and all men
had heard the voice of those who preached it, and when
the trophies of the martyrs' contests had been raised
everywhere, witnessing more gloriously than words to the
true Godhead of Christ. Though he had heard thousands
of words and seen many heroes and miracles he still
persisted in his error and preferred falsehood to truth. But
when he had been baptized, and in a mock ceremony at
that, he was not only at once a Christian but joined the
very choir of the martyrs. Being a mime, on the stage he
had ventured on this reckless deed in order to excite laughter.
He mimiked the washing and baptized himself on the
stage, proclaiming the Trinity. The spectators laughed at
the act, but for him his act was no longer laughable nor
play-acting, but a real birth and a re-creation, and the very
thing that the Mystery is. He went out with the soul of
a martyr instead of that of a mime, with a noble body as
though trained for wisdom and hard labours, and a tongue
which provoked the tyrant's anger instead of his laughter.
Thus he who throughout his life had been mocking became
serious, and became so eager for Christ that he gladly died
after suffering many tortures, that he might not deny his
love even by his tongue.

Gelasius too came to love Christ and know Him in this
way. Apparently he approached with a mind full of hate
and hostility, but when He whom he had fought opened
the eye of his soul and showed him His own beauty he
was at once beside himself over that beauty and displayed
the reverse attitude, and instead of an enemy became a
lover. That love is an ecstasy because it leads those whom

it seizes beyond the limits of human nature. This the prophet points out in the things which he addresses to Christ concerning His cross and death, saying "many shall be amazed at Thee": "just as many shall be amazed at Thee, so Thy beauty shall be marred from men, even from the sons of man" (Is. 52:14 LXX).

The noble Ardalion too was baptized in mockery that he might please the spectators. He was a clown and a professional in related pleasures for those who frequent them. But he was baptized, imitating the Saviour's passion not by symbols or images but in very deed. He enacted the good confession of the martyrs and was hung up upon a cross naked by other actors in mockery. But when he proclaimed Christ and felt the wounds he suddenly changed his mind and his soul joined with his voice and his will followed that which he imitated. Now he was truly what he called himself in the act, a Christian. So great was the effect of the mocking wounds and the pretended voice that he at once began to love Christ. Because he said that he loved Christ, the fire of love spread to his heart as though it had been blown thither from his mouth. For other men the good proceeds to the mouth "from the good treasure of the heart" (Mt. 12:35), but for Ardalion the treasure of floods above flowed to the heart from his mouth.

O ineffable power of Christ! Not by conferring benefits or bestowing crowns, nor by by attracting him by the hope of good things, but by receiving him as a sharer in His wounds and dishonour He laid hold on him and attached him, so that He persuaded him of the things which he formerly could not bear even to hear. At once he broke away from long-standing, deep-rooted habit; he changed his will to the most contrary disposition. He changed his course from the most evil and wicked of all to the best of all; for nothing could be meaner than a mime or more philosophical than a martyr. What have they in common? How does it follow by natural reason that wounds and dishonour should engender love? And that the enemy should be captured and vanquished by the very things by which he showed hostility and which would give cause to the faithful to flee from Christianity? Who when suffering pains would by them be glad to inspire love in one who had sought to show hatred, with the effect of making him a friend and supporter instead of a bitter enemy and persecutor?

So then the word of teaching seems to have had no effect. The power of Baptism brought it all about. Ardalion had heard the words of our common salvation; he had seen miracles, since many martyrs had boldly borne their witness in his time. Nevertheless he was still blind and hostile towards the light until he was baptized and received the brands of Christ and "made the good confession" (1 Tim. 6:13). For this is the end of Baptism, to imitate the witness of Christ under Pilate and His perseverance until the cross and death. Baptism is an imitation by means of symbols and images of these sacred acts, but also—for those who have the opportunity to risk their lives to show their religion—by the very same acts themselves.

[§ 18.   Baptism as a personal experience of God]

Many are the remedies which down through the ages have been devised for this sick race; it was Christ's death alone which was able to bring true life and health. For this reason, to be born by this new birth and live the blessed life and be disposed to health and, as far as lies in man, to confess the faith and take on oneself the passion and die the death of Christ, is nothing less than to drink of this medicine. This is the power of the new law; thus it is that a Christian is born. In this way he arrives at admirable wisdom and undertakes the noblest deeds. His faith is unmovable, since he believes without compulsion and governs his conduct by the power of God, and not by laws. Holding fast both faith and virtue he is formed by both into the blessed likeness of Christ. "The kingdom of God," it is said, "does not consist in words but in power" (1 Cor. 4:20), and "the word of the cross is to us who are being saved the power of God" (1 Cor. 1:18).

The new law, then, is spiritual because the Spirit works everything. The former law is written because it goes no further than letters and sounds. Therefore that law is "a shadow" (Heb. 10:1) and an image, the present one is reality and truth. The words and letters are like an image in relation to reality. Before they were realized God foreshadowed them on many occasions by the tongue of the prophets. "I will make," He says, "a new covenant, not like the covenant which I made with their fathers" (Jer. 31:31-32). What does this mean? "This," He says, "is the covenant which I will make with the house of Israel and the house of Judah: I will put my laws within their mind and in their hearts I will write them" (Jer. 31:33)—that is, not composing them by mere sound of words, but by the Lawgiver's presence, without intermediary. For He says, "no longer shall each man teach his neighbour and each his brother, saying, 'Know the Lord,' for they shall all know me, from the least of them to the greatest" (Jer. 31:34). Because he had obtained this law David also uttered this blessed saying, "I know that the Lord is great" (Ps. 135:5). He says, "I know," having experienced it himself, not by having heard it taught by others. Wherefore he leads others too to the same experience, saying, "O taste and see that the Lord is gracious" (Ps. 34:9). Even though the blessed man had praised God's graciousness in many and varied words, yet, since the words were not capable of showing the reality, he himself summons his listeners to the experience of the things which he praises.

[§ 19. How this experience engenders
love for Him]

It is this experience which the washing imparts to the souls of those who are being baptized. It makes the creature to know the Creator, the mind to know the Truth, the desire to know Him who alone is desirable. For this reason the longing is great, the love ineffable, and the desire beyond measure. There is nothing which the washing lacks; all things agree with it, nothing is contrary to it—in addition, it is all abundance.

Let us examine this further. God has emplanted the desire into our souls by which every need should lead to the attainment of that which is good, every thought to the attainment of truth. For these we long in their purity: good rather than evil, truth rather than error; for no one enjoys being deceived or is pleased by going astray and meeting with evil instead of good. Yet no one by desiring them has ever attained them in their purity. What is good and true in our eyes does not correspond to the name, but rather the contrary. Thus it is also clear that neither is the power of our love nor the the the greatness of our joy apparent when the things which we must love and which we enjoy are absent, nor is the compulsion of desire or the ardour of its fire known when the object of desire is absent.

For those who have tasted of the Saviour, the Object of desire is present. From the beginning human desire was made to be gauged and measured by the desire for Him, and is a treasury so great, so ample, that it is able to encompass even God. Thus there is no satisfaction, nothing stills the desire, even if men attain to all the excellent things in life, for we still thirst as though we had none of the things for which we long. The thirst of human souls needs, as it were, an infinite water; how then could this limited world suffice?

This is what the Lord hinted when He said to the Samaritan woman, "he who drinks of this water will thirst again, but whoever drinks of the water that I shall give him will never thirst (Jn. 4:13-14). This is the water that slakes the thirst of human souls, for it says, "when I behold Thy glory I shall be satisfied with it" (Ps. 17:15 LXX). The eye was created capable of perceiving light, the ear for sound, and each member for its appropriate end; the desire of the soul has for its object Christ alone.

He, then, is its repose because He alone is goodness and truth and anything else it desires. Those, therefore, who attain to Him are hindered by nothing from loving to the extent that love was implanted into our souls from the beginning, or from rejoicing as much as human nature is able to rejoice, or from anything that virtue and the water of regeneration added to these faculties. Since the good things of ordinary life are not true to their name it is impossible for either desire or joy to be fully effective in them, for even if something seems to be beautiful it is but a paltry spectre of true beauty.* But in this case, since there is nothing which will stand in the way, love is clearly shown to be wondrous and ineffable and joy to be beyond description. Above all this is so because God has ordained each of these passions with Himself as its object, so that we should love Him and find our joy in Him alone. It follows, I think, that the passion should be in proportion to that infinite goodness and thus, so to speak, be in keeping with it.

Let us then examine how great love is. This is the proof of its richness, that for all the benefits which He bestows on us He esteems love to be the sole recompense, and if He receives this at our hands He repays all our debt. Wherefore, since it is a compensation for infinite benefits in the sight of God our Judge, how can it fail to be exceedingly great? It is clear that joy in every way corresponds to the abundance of love. Delight is in all things adequate to the affection, and the greatest joy follows the greatest love. It is apparent, then, that human souls have a great and wondrous capacity for love and joy, and that it is perfectly employed only when He is present who is truly lovable as well as beloved. This is what the Saviour calls joy that is fulfilled (cf. Jn. 15:11, 16:24, 17:13).

For this reason, when the Spirit has come to anyone and given of His fruits through His indwelling, love and joy hold the first place among them. "For the fruit of the Spirit," Paul says, "is love, joy . . ." (Gal. 5:22). Therefore, when God comes to our souls He grants these first of all as a perception of Himself. When one becomes aware of

---

*A reminiscence of the platonic doctrine of ideas, in which beautiful things are mere pale reflections of the "idea" or prototype of Beauty, eternally existing.

the good, one necessarily loves it and rejoices in it. When
He appeared to men in bodily form He first of all sought
from us that we should recognize Him. It was this that He
taught and straightway brought about; indeed, it was for
this reason that He went so far as to become perceptible,
and for the sake of this He accomplished all things. "For
this," He says, "I was born and for this I have come into
the world, to bear witness to the truth" (Jn. 18:37). Since
He Himself is the Truth, He all but said, "that I might
declare Myself." This is what He now does as He comes
to those who are being baptized. He witnesses to the truth
by casting out that which merely seems to be good; He
brings in the truth by showing it and, as He Himself says,
by "manifesting Himself to them" (Jn. 14:22).

[§ 20.   The testimony of Saint John Chrysostom to this effect]

From the very acts themselves, as I have stated, it
appears that it is true that those who are being washed
in Baptism receive some experience of God. If we need
witnesses, there are many who were beloved by God. Let
one above all suffice as he comes forward on behalf of
them all, John [Chrysostom] who has a soul more radiant
than the sunbeam and a voice more brilliant than gold.
We must cite the words of that goodly tongue (Homily 7,
on 2 Cor.):

> What does it mean that, 'beholding the glory of the Lord
> we are being changed into the same likeness' (2 Cor. 3:1)?
> This was shown more clearly when the gifts of miraculous signs
> were active; yet for him who has believing eyes it is even now
> not difficult to observe. For as soon as we are baptized the soul,
> being cleansed by the Spirit, shines more brightly than the sun.
> Nor do we only contemplate God's glory, we also receive this
> brightness. It is as when pure silver is exposed to the sunbeam;
> it itself becomes shining not merely because of its own nature,
> but due to the brightness of the sun. Thus also when the soul is
> cleansed and has become brighter than all silver it receives the
> ray of light from the glory of the Spirit so that such a glory may
> be produced in it as can come only from the Lord the Spirit.

A little later he writes:

> Do you wish that I show you this more evidently from the
> apostles? Consider Paul, whose garment had power (Acts 19:12),
> and Peter, whose shadow even was mighty (Acts 5:12). Had they
> not borne the image of the King and reflected light unapproachable,
> would their garments and their shadows have had such power?
> The robes of a king inspire awe even in bandits. Do you wish
> to see this glory shining even through the body? 'Gazing at the
> face of Stephen,' it says, 'they saw that it was like the face of an
> angel' (Acts 6:15). But this is nothing compared to the glory
> flashing from within like lightning. That which Moses of old had
> on his face the apostles bore upon their souls, indeed to a far
> higher degree. That of Moses was more perceptible, but this is
> incorporeal. Just as fiery particles from radiant bodies pass to
> other bodies close to them and impart to them of their own bright-
> ness, so it happens in the case of the faithful also. For this reason
> those who have experienced this separate themselves from earth
> and are absorbed in dreams of heavenly things. Woe is me! It
> would be good to groan bitterly! Though we enjoy such a noble
> estate we do not even know of what we speak because the things
> are quickly lost and we are attracted towards the things which our
> senses perceive. This ineffable and awesome glory remains in us
> for a day or two, but then we extinguish it by bringing upon
> it the winter of everyday affairs and repelling the sunbeams by the
> denseness of the clouds.

[§ 21.   How Baptism is an illumination]

It is therefore not merely to the extent of reasoning,
thinking, and believing that the baptized may know God;
something far greater and closer to reality may be found
in these waters. To think of that flash of light in terms
of infusing this knowledge into the mind and enlightening
the intellect would not be reasonable. It vanishes after a
day or two when the crowds and confusions press upon the
newly initiated. As for one's faith, no one loses knowledge
of it merely by being overwhelmed with cares in so short
a time. It is possible to have weighty cares and yet to be
an able theologian and, what is worse, to be subject to evil
passions and be conversant with the word of salvation and
true philosophy!

Accordingly it is clear that this knowledge is an immediate
perception of God, since the ray that comes from Him

invisibly kindles the very soul. Of this ray the trappings of the baptismal washing are symbols. All things are full of brightness: the torches, the chants, the choirs, the processions, nothing that is not radiant, with the baptismal robes all resplendent and prepared for a spectacle of light. The covering for the head depicts the very Spirit and bears the pattern of His coming in a symbol. It is made in the form of a tongue, and preserves the form in which the Spirit appeared when He at the beginning baptized the apostles. For then He lighted upon the head of each of them as fire in the form of a tongue. The reason why He descended in the form of a tongue was, in my opinion, that He had come to interpret the Logos* who is akin to Him and to teach Him to those who knew Him not. It is the office of a tongue to be the messenger of the invisible thoughts of the mind and to manifest what is within. So the Logos proclaims the Father who generated Him, while the Spirit proclaims the Son. Thus Christ said to the Father, "I glorified Thee" (Jn. 17:4), while of the Paraclete He said, "He will glorify Me" (Jn. 16:14). This then is the reason why He appeared to them in this way.

That symbol points out to us that miracle, that memory, that beautiful day which saw the beginning of Baptism, that we might know that those on whom the Spirit first came imparted Him to those who came after. They, in turn, imparted Him to those who came after them, and thus He has come step by step as far as ourselves. That gift will never fail until He who supplies it returns to us openly in His Person. Then the Master will grant to the blessed ones a pure vision of Himself after removing all things that stand in the way. At present, however, it is only through the veil of gross flesh that it is possible for them to see Him.

The fruit of the perception of the blessed is unutterable joy and extraordinary love. Theirs is to perform great and virtuous deeds and to accomplish wondrous works, so that

---

*The "Word" of Jn. 1:1—but with many overtones of meaning such as "reason" not conveyed by the English term.

they pass through all things triumphant and crowned with victory. Armed with these weapons of love and joy it was impossible for the saints to be overcome either by terrors or pleasures. Joy prevailed over miseries, pleasures were incapable of drawing aside or destroying those who were held together and bound to Him by so great a power of affection.

[§ 22.   Summary: The effects of Baptism]

These are therefore the effects of Baptism: to set free from sins, to reconcile man to God, to make man one with God, to open the eyes that souls might perceive the divine ray—in sum, to prepare for the life to come. Therefore we do right when we give it the name of "birth" and other names which have the same meaning, as well as those which indicate that it causes the knowledge of God to rise as a sun for the souls of those who are being initiated. It is life, and a foundation and root of life, since the Saviour has defined eternal life as consisting of "knowing the only true God and Jesus Christ whom He has sent" (Jn. 17:3), just as Solomon said before Him, "to know Thee is the root of immortality" (Wis. 15:3).

To add a proof from reason (if we must!)—who does not know that man's true nature and superiority consist of reasoning and knowing? But if man's nature consists of reasoning and knowing, it would consist in the best knowledge of all, free from error. What fairer knowledge could there be, and purer from error, than to know God Himself, when He Himself opens the eye of the soul and turns it to Himself? It is this which is the fruit of Baptism.

By all that has been said it has been demonstrated that the Mystery [of Baptism] is the beginning of the life in Christ, and causes men to exist, live, and excel in true life and being. Yet if these effects do not follow in the case of all who are baptized it is not right to condemn the Mystery. The calamity must be attributed to those who have been initiated, either because they have not been well disposed towards the gift of grace, or else because they have abandoned the treasure. How much more just it is to lay the blame for this discrepancy on the initiates themselves who have misused their Baptism, rather than blame the initiation which is one and the same for all, for the things which are contrary to it!

It is evident that the abundance of blessings afore-mentioned is due neither to nature nor to personal effort, but is the effect of Baptism. But if the contrary results, is it not absurd to suppose that the same thing could both bring illumination and not bring it, at the same time make men heavenly and make them in no way superior to that which is earthly? We would not blame the sun or condemn it as invisible because all do not see its rays. Rather, we should bring in the verdict of those who see! Neither should we be acting reasonably were we to attribute to the illumination any effect except that from which it derives its name.

THE THIRD BOOK

What the holy chrism contributes

[§ 1. How Scripture links the gift of the Spirit
with anointing and imposition of hands]

It would be fitting, then, that those who are thus
spiritually created and begotten should obtain an energy
suitable to such a birth, and a corresponding animation.
This the sacred rite of the most divine chrism accomplishes
for us. It activates the spiritual energies, one in one man,
another in another, or even several at the same time,
depending on how each man is prepared for this Mystery.

Those who have been washed experience that which
took place in the first ages when the hands of the apostles
were laid on those whom they had baptized. Scripture
says that the Spirit was given when the apostles laid hands
upon those who had been initiated. Now too the Paraclete
comes upon those who are being chrismated.

These are the proofs. First, the ancient law anointed
kings and priests; likewise the Church's ordinance anoints
kings and lays hands upon priests and in both cases invokes
the grace of the Holy Spirit. This indicates that both the
former and the latter have the same intent and the same
power. Secondly, they share their names, the former name

being "anointing," and the latter "communication of the Spirit." The holiest of the priests style the ordination of priests "anointing," and again they pray that those on whom they confer the Mystery of the chrism may become partakers of the Holy Spirit and believe that they are. When they expound to those who are being initiated what the rite is, they call it "the seal of the spiritual gift," for this is what they pronounce over those who are being chrismated.*

[§ 2.   How Christ Himself was anointed with the Holy Spirit]

Further, Christ the Lord was Himself anointed, not by receiving chrism poured on the head, but by receiving the Holy Spirit. For the sake of the flesh which He had assumed He became the treasury of all spiritual energy. He is not only Christ [the Anointed One] but also Chrism [anointing], for it says, ""Your name is as ointment poured forth" (Cant. 1:3). The latter He is from the beginning, the other He becomes afterwards. As long as that by which God would impart His own did not exist, He was the Chrism and remained in Himself. Afterwards the blessed flesh was created which received the entire fulness of the Godhead (Col. 1:19). To it, as John says, "God did not give the Spirit by measure" (Jn. 3:34), but He infused into Him His entire living riches. It was then that the Chrism was poured forth into that flesh, so it is now called the Anointed. By being imparted to the flesh the divine Chrism Himself was poured forth.

He did not change place, nor did He penetrate or pass over a wall, but, as He Himself showed, He left no barrier standing which could separate us from Him. Since God occupies every place He was not separated from man by place, but by man's being at variance with Him. Our nature separated itself from God by being contrary to Him in

---

*The formula at the Chrismation, immediately after Baptism, is "The seal of the gift of the Holy Spirit."

everything that it possessed and by having nothing in common with Him. God remained Himself alone; our nature was man, and no more.

When, however, flesh was deified and human nature gained possession of God Himself by hypostatic union,* the former barrier opposed to God became joined to the Chrism. The difference gave way when God became man, thus removing the separation between Godhead and manhood. So chrism represents Christ as the point of contact between both natures; there could be no point of contact were they still separate.

[§ 3. How Christ is the Source of our spiritual anointing]

It is, therefore, as though the vessel of alabaster (cf. Mk. 14:3) were by some means to become the chrism it contains. The chrism would then no longer not be imparted to those outside, it would no longer remain within the box or by itself. In the same way, when our nature is deified in the Saviour's Body, nothing separates the human race from God. Accordingly there is nothing but sin that hinders us from participating in His graces. Now since the barrier was twofold, consisting on the one hand in diversity of nature, on the other in a will corrupted by evil, the Saviour has removed the one by becoming incarnate, the other by being crucified.

The cross released us from sin. Since Baptism then has the efficacy of His cross and death, we go forward to the chrism, the participation in the Spirit. When both the barriers have been removed there is nothing which prevents the Holy Spirit from being "poured out upon all flesh" (Joel 2:28, Acts 2:17)—that is, as far as this life can bear it, for death is yet a third barrier to the dwelling together with God and does not permit those who still wear the mortal body to go beyond the dim reflection as of a mirror (1 Cor. 13:12).

---

*I.e., in the Person of the Incarnate Lord.

Therefore, though men were triply separated from God—
by nature, by sin, and by death—yet the Saviour made them
to attain to Him perfectly and to be immediately united
to Him by successively removing all obstacles. The first
barrier He removed by partaking of manhood, the second
by being put to death on the cross. As for the final barrier,
the tyranny of death, He eliminated it completely from our
nature by rising again. For this reason Paul says, "the last
enemy to be destroyed is death" (1 Cor. 15:26). He would
not have called it an enemy unless it were an obstacle to
our true happiness. It is necessary that the heirs of the
immortal God should be set free from corruption, for Paul
says, "corruption does not inherit incorruption" (1 Cor.
15:50). After the common resurrection of mankind of which
the Saviour's resurrection is the cause, the "mirror" and the
"dimness" (1 Cor. 13:12) recede [into oblivion] and those
who have been purified in heart shall see God face to face
(Mt. 5:8).

[§ 4.   How Chrismation confers the gifts of the Holy Spirit]

So the effect of this sacred rite is the imparting of the
energies of the Holy Spirit. The chrism brings in the Lord
Jesus Himself, in whom is man's whole salvation and all
hope of benefits. From Him we receive the participation in
the Holy Spirit and "through Him we have access to the
Father" (Eph. 2:18). While the Trinity in common is the
Artificer of the re-creation of men it is the Logos alone
who effects it. Not only while He dwelt among men did
He share their nature with them and, as Paul says, "was
offered to bear the sins of many" (Heb. 9:28), but it is
for ever afterwards that He wears our nature. Therefore
"we have Him as an advocate with God" (1 Jn. 2:1).
Through Himself "He purifies our conscience from dead
works" (Heb. 9:14); through Himself He gives the Spirit.

In the earliest times this Mystery conferred on those
who had been baptized gifts of healing, prophecy, tongues

and such like, which provided a clear proof to all men of
the extraordinary power of Christ. Of these there was need
when Christianity was being planted and godliness was being
established. From that source even now such gifts have been
imparted to some. Even in our own and in most recent times
men have spoken of future events, have cast out demons
and have healed diseases by prayer alone. Nor was it only
while they were still walking about alive that they were
able to do this, but since the spiritual energy has not departed
from the blessed ones even after death their very tombs have
availed to do the same.

But the gifts which the chrism always procures for
Christians and which are always timely are the gifts of
godliness, prayer, love, and sobriety, and the other gifts
which are opportune for those who receive them. Yet they
elude many Christians; the greatness and the power of
this Mystery is hidden from them and, as it is written in
the Acts, "they did not even know that there is a Holy
Spirit" (19:2). Since this Mystery takes place in infancy
they have no perception of its gifts when it is celebrated
and they receive them; when they have reached maturity
they have turned aside to what they ought not to do and
have blinded the eye of the soul.

Yet in truth the Spirit imparts His own gifts to those
who are being initiated, "apportioning to each individually
as He wills" (1 Cor. 12:11). Nor has the Master ceased
from doing us good, since He has promised to be with us
until the end. The sacred rite, then, is not an empty thing.
Just as we receive the remission of sins from the awesome
washing and the Body of Christ from the sacred table, and
these things will not cease until He who is their beginning
Himself visibly returns, so likewise it is altogether necessary
that Christians should enjoy what belongs to the most divine
Chrismation and partake of the gifts of the Holy Spirit. How
would it be consistent if some of the sacred rites should be
efficacious and this one be of no avail? Or that in their
case, as Paul says, "He who promised is faithful" (Heb.
10:23), but in the case of this rite He should be dubious?
We must condemn none of them, or else condemn

the others as well, since the same power is at work through them all, with the one immolation of the one Lamb, His death, His Blood, conferring perfection on them all.

The Holy Spirit, therefore, is truly given. To some He is given that they may be able to benefit others and, as Paul says, "edify the Church" (1 Cor. 14:4) by speaking of the future or by teaching mysteries or by freeing men from diseases with a single word. To others, however, He is given in order that they themselves may become more virtuous and shine with godliness or with an abundance of sobriety, love, or humility.

It is possible, then, to practise sobriety by using reason and morality, and to train one's character in righteousness and to become virtuous in other ways by prayer and love. Further, one whose will is moved by God is able to control passion and to practice love of fellow man and justice and to display whatever else belongs to wisdom. Just as there are beastly vices in those who are under the influence of evil spirits so, contrariwise, there are divine virtues which surpass human convention when God Himself moves a man. In this way it was that the blessed Paul loved, that David was humble, and that others displayed praiseworthy qualities beyond what is proper to man. Paul wrote to the Philippians that he loved them "with the affection of Jesus Christ" (Phil. 1:8), while of David God says, "I have found a man after my heart" (1 Sam. 13:14, Acts 13:22).

Faith indeed also is a spiritual gift. This the Saviour's apostles pray that they may receive, saying, "increase our faith" (Lk. 17:5). He Himself prays for their sanctification from the Father when He says, "Sanctify them in Thy truth" (Jn. 17:17), and God grants Him the petition as He prays. The saying, "the Spirit Himself intercedes for us with sighs too deep for words" (Rom. 8:26), seems to me to supply strength to prayer.

To sum up the matter—to those to whom He imparts of His own gifts, the Holy Spirit is "the Spirit of wisdom and understanding, the Spirit of counsel and might and of godliness" (Is. 11:2), and of the other gifts of which He bears the name.

[§ 5.   The efficacy of the holy chrism]

On all, then, who have been initiated the Mystery produces its proper effects. Not all, however, have perception of the gifts or eagerness to make use of the riches which they have been given. Some are unable to grasp the gifts because of their immature age, others are not eager because they are not prepared or have failed to give effect to their preparation. Some have subsequently repented and bewailed the sins which they have committed and live according to right reason, and so have given proof of the grace that has been infused into their souls. Accordingly Paul writes to Timothy, "do not neglect the gift you have" (1 Tim. 4:14). Thus it does not profit us to have received the gift if we are careless. There is need of effort and vigilance on the part of those who wish to have these things active in their souls.

If then one of the righteous appears to excel in love, in purity and self-control, in abundant humility or piety, or in any such thing above what is common to man, it ought to be ascribed to the most divine Chrismation. We should thus believe that the gift was bestowed on him when he partook of the Mystery and that it became active afterwards.

The same is true of those who speak plainly of things to come, and of those who without any artifice heal those who are of unsound mind or suffer from other diseases, as well as those who exhibit other gifts—they have them because they have received them from the Mystery. If, on the one hand, the celebration of the Mystery does not make those who receive it active at the time with spiritual energies, or, on the other hand, we fail to attribute subsequent spiritual accomplishments to the Mystery, why is it then necessary to undergo it? Further, if the initiation of the divine Chrismation is incapable of conferring that for which it is sought, what would be its benefit?

Nor, if we cannot enjoy the special gifts of Chrismation, can we reasonably claim that the rite might be capable of helping us in some other way. If it does not enable the recipient to obtain the things which are promised and to which it all refers, for which the officiant prays and which he teaches the candidate that he is about to receive, it is hardly possible to expect any other benefit from it. But if the Mystery is not in vain—for nothing else that is Christian is in vain, as Paul says: "our preaching is not in vain, nor is your faith in vain" (1 Cor. 15:14)—then if any spiritual energy belonging to the compass of graces derived from it may be found among men, it must be referred to those prayers and to the sacred Chrismation.

In short, then, there is nothing whatever, there is no benefit which is available to men by their reconciliation with God, which has not been bestowed through Him who has been appointed the Mediator between God and man. He has given us no other means whatever by which we may find the Mediator and lay hold of Him and receive what is His than the Mysteries. They make us His kinsmen in His Blood, partakers of the graces which He received through His flesh, and partakers of the suffering which He endured.

[§ 6.   The Sacraments as means of
our salvation]

Two things, then, commend us to God, and in them lies all the salvation of men. The first is that we be initiated into the most sacred Mysteries, the second, that we train the will for virtue. Human endeavour can have no other function that that of preserving what has been given so as not to waste the treasure: consequently, the power of the Mysteries alone bestows on us all these blessings. Of the various rites each has its own effect; participation of the Spirit and of His gifts depends on the most holy chrism. Therefore, while one may not be able to demonstrate the spiritual gift at the very time that the sacred rite takes place, but only much later, we should not be ignorant of the cause and origin of the power. The illumination of Baptism is introduced into the souls of those who have been initiated as soon as they have been washed, yet it is not at the time evident to all. For some of the virtuous it appears after a time and through much sweat and toil when they have cleansed the eye of the soul by the love of Christ.

It is on account of this chrism that the houses of prayer help us to pray. They become for us what they are called by being anointed with chrism. The chrism poured forth is a helper for us with God the Father because of the very fact that Christ has emptied Himself (cf. Phil. 2:8) and become an anointing [chrism] and has been poured forth as far as our very nature. As for the altars, they imitate the Saviour's hand. From the anointed table we receive the bread as from that undefiled hand, receiving the Body of Christ and drinking His Blood like those whom the Master first made partakers of the sacred table as He pledged them with that awesome cup of friendship.

[§ 7. Summary: Chrismation makes us partakers of Christ, the Anointed One]

Since, then, the same One is both Priest and Altar, Sacrifice and Offerer, the One through Whom He offers and that which He offers,* He divided the functions among the Mysteries, assigning one thing to the bread of blessing, another to the chrism. The Saviour is Altar and Offerer by virtue of the chrism. The altar became an altar at the beginning by being anointed, and in the case of the priests it was by being anointed that they were priests. Christ is a sacrifice by virtue of the cross and death because He died for the glory of God the Father. We proclaim, Paul says, His death as often as we eat this bread (1 Cor. 11:26). Furthermore, Christ is the chrism and the anointing through the Holy Spirit. While therefore He could perform the most sacred acts and sanctify, yet He as God could not Himself

---

*Compare the prayer at the Great Entrance—"Thou art the Offerer and the Offered, the Acceptor and the Distributed, O Christ our God"—in the Liturgy of St. John Chrysostom.

undergo sanctification. The power of sanctification belongs to the altar and to him who sacrifices and offers, but not to that which is offered and sacrificed, since the altar is spoken of as sanctifying, for He says, "the altar makes the gift sacred" (Mt. 23:19). He is the bread by virtue of the flesh which is sanctified and deified, and which has received both the anointing and the stripes. "The bread," He says, "which I shall give is my flesh." "Which I shall give" means in sacrifice "for the life of the world" (Jn. 6:51).

It is as bread, therefore, that He is offered. It is as chrism that He offers, in that He has deified His own flesh and received us as partakers of the anointing. Jacob showed the type of these things and dedicated the stone to God after he had anointed it (Gen. 28:18); it was by anointing it that he offered it. By the stone he alluded to the flesh of the Saviour, which is the chief cornerstone (Eph. 2:20) on which the true Israel, the Mind who alone knows the Father (cf. 1 Cor. 2:10), poured forth the Chrism of His Godhead. Or else he hinted at us, whom He Himself will raise up from the stones as children for Abraham (Mt. 3:9) by bestowing the anointing. The Holy Spirit who has been poured forth on those who have been anointed is, among other things, also the Spirit of adoption and, as it says, "bears witness with our spirit that we are children of God" and "cries in our hearts 'Abba, Father'" (Rom. 8:16, 15).

It is in such ways that the most divine chrism helps those who resolve to live in Christ.

THE FOURTH BOOK

How Holy Communion contributes to our salvation

[§ 1.   The greatest of all the Mysteries]

After the Chrismation we go to the table. This is the perfection of the life in Christ; for those who attain it there is nothing lacking for the blessedness which they seek. It is no longer death and the tomb and a participation in the better life which we receive, but the risen One Himself. Nor do we receive such gifts of the Spirit as we may, but the very Benefactor Himself, the very Temple whereon is founded the whole compass of graces.

Now indeed Christ is present in each of the Mysteries. It is with Himself that we are anointed and washed; He also is our Feast. He is present with those who are being initiated and imparts His gifts to them. The mode, however, is not entirely the same. As He washes them in Baptism He cleanses them from the filth of wickedness and imposes His own form upon them; when He anoints them He activates the energies of the Spirit of which He, for the sake of our flesh, became the Treasury. But when He has led the initiate to the table and has given him His Body to eat He entirely changes him, and transforms him into His own state. The clay is no longer clay when it has received the royal likeness but is already the Body of the King.* It is impossible to conceive of anything more blessed than this.

It is therefore the final Mystery as well, since it is not possible to go beyond it or to add anything to it. The first Mystery [Baptism] clearly needs the middle one [Chrismation], and that in turn stands in need of the final Mystery. After the Eucharist then, there is nowhere further to go. There we must stand, and try to examine the means by which we may preserve the treasure to the end.

Now then, when we were baptized the Mystery achieved for us all that belonged to it, but we were not yet perfect. We were without the gifts of the Spirit which depend on the most holy chrism. For those who had been baptized by Philip (Acts 8:12) the Holy Spirit was not yet present to bestow these graces, but in addition to Baptism the hands of John and Peter were needed, for as it says, "He had not fallen on any of them, but they had only been baptized in the name of the Lord Jesus. Then they laid their hands on them and they received the Holy Spirit" (Acts 8:16-17).

When we have obtained this and the sacred rite has displayed its power in us we possess the grace which has been given. Yet it is by no means inevitable that our subsequent life be in keeping with the Benefactor. We may well incur punishment. Even without destroying what has been given nothing prevents one from having been initiated in the Mystery and yet being deficient in that which is needful.

Of this there are many witnesses. It happened to some Corinthians while the apostles were yet living. They were filled with the Spirit, they prophesied, spoke with tongues, and displayed other gifts; yet so far were they from being in a divine and spiritual state that they were beset with envy and untimely ambition, with strife and suchlike evils. For these things Paul blames them when he says, "you are of the flesh and behaving like ordinary men" (1 Cor. 3:3). Even though they were spiritual in terms of participating in

---

*By receiving Christ's sacramental Body we are incorporated into His mystical Body, and thus become His Body.

divine graces, yet it did not suffice them for casting out all evil from the soul.

In the case of the Eucharist there is none of these evils. In those in whom the Bread of Life has produced the effects by which they have warded off death no evil is present as they partake of the feast, nor do they introduce any, nor may they be accused thereof. It is not at all possible for this mystic rite to be wholly efficacious and have those who are its initiates share in any wickedness whatever.

[§ 2.   How the Eucharist completes Baptism and Chrismation]

Why is this? Because the efficacy of this mystic rite consists in this, that those who are consecrated thereby should lack none of its fruits. In accordance with His promise we dwell in Christ by means of the feast and Christ dwells in us, for He says, "he abides in me, and I in him" (Jn. 6:57).

But when Christ dwells in us, what else is needed, or what benefit escapes us? When we dwell in Christ, what else will we desire? He dwells in us, and He is our dwelling place. How blessed are we by reason of this dwelling place, how blessed are we that we have become a dwelling for such a one as He! What good thing is lacking for those who are in such a state? What have they to do with wickedness who have entered into such brightness? What evil can withstand so great an abundance of good? What evil thing can continue to be present or enter from without when Christ is so evidently with us and completely penetrates and surrounds us?

By placing Himself as a shield on every side He prevents the darts which are hurled at us from without from touching us, since He is our dwelling place. If there is anything wicked within He thrusts it away and expels it, for He dwells within the house and wholly fills it with Himself. That of which we partake is not something of His, but Himself. It is not some ray and light which we receive in our souls, but the

very orb of the sun. So we dwell in Him and are indwelt
and become one spirit with Him. The soul and the body
and all their faculties forthwith become spiritual, for our
souls, our bodies and blood, are united with His.

What is the result? The more excellent things overcome
the inferior, things divine prevail over the human, and that
takes place which Paul says concerning the resurrection,
"what is mortal is swallowed up by life" (2 Cor. 5:4),
and further, "it is no longer I who live, but Christ who
lives in me" (Gal. 2:20).

O how great are the Mysteries! What a thing it is for
Christ's mind to be mingled with ours, our will to be blended
with His, our body with His Body and our blood with His
Blood! What is our mind when the divine mind obtains
control? What is our will when that blessed will has overcome
it? What is our dust when it has been overpowered by His
fire?

That these things are so Paul shows when he claims that
he has neither his own mind nor will nor life, but that all
these have become Christ's for him. He states, "we have the
mind of Christ" (2 Cor. 2:16), and "you desire proof that
Christ is speaking in me" (2 Cor. 13:3), and "I yearn for
you all with the affection of Christ Jesus" (Phil. 1:18).
From this it is clear that he has the same will as Christ.
To sum it all up, "it is no longer I who live, but Christ
lives in me" (Gal. 2:20).

[§ 3.   The Eucharist perfects the other Mysteries]

So perfect is this Mystery, so far does it excel every other
sacred rite that it leads to the very summit of good things.
Here also is the final goal of every human endeavour. For
in it we obtain God Himself, and God is united with us
in the most perfect union, for what attachment can be more
complete than to become one spirit with God?

Wherefore the Eucharist, alone of sacred rites, supplies
perfection to the other Mysteries. In the act of initiating
it comes to their aid, since they cannot be completed otherwise.

It assists the initiates after their initiation, when the ray of light derived from the Mysteries must be revived after having been obscured by the darkness of sins. To revive those who fade away and die because of their sins is the work of the sacred table alone.

[§ 4. Excursus—Christ's atoning work]

When a man has fallen it is not possible for him to be raised by human power, nor can human evil be destroyed by human righteousness. The commission of sin involves injury to God Himself, for it says, "you dishonour God by breaking the law" (Rom. 2:23). There is need of virtue greater than is found in man to be able to cancel the indictment.

For the lowest it is particularly easy to commit an injury against Him who is greatest. Yet it is impossible for him to compensate for this insolence by any honour, particularly when he is in many ways indebted to Him whom he has injured, and He who is injured is so far superior that the distance between them cannot even be measured. He, then, who seeks to cancel the indictment against himself must restore the honour to Him who has been insulted and repay more than he owes, partly by way of restitution, partly by adding a compensation for the wrong which he has done. Yet how can he who is unable even to attain to the measure of his debts succeed in surpassing it?

It was therefore impossible for any man to reconcile himself to God by introducing his own righteousness. Accordingly neither could the old law overcome the enmity, nor would the unaided efforts of those who live under the new be capable of achieving this peace, since both the former and the latter are works of men's own power and of human righteousness. The very law itself Paul calls human righteousness, for in speaking of the old law he says, "they did not submit to God's righteousness, seeking to establish their own" (Rom. 10:3). Its effectiveness against

our evil condition was limited to this alone, to prepare us
for health and to make us fit for the Physician's hand. So
he says, "the law was our custodian until Christ came"
(Gal. 3:24). Similarly blessed John [the Baptist] baptized
in anticipation of Him who was to come; and all the
philosophy of men and all their labour for true righteousness
are no more than preliminaries and preparations.

Wherefore, since we by our own means and of ourselves
were unable to display righteousness, Christ Himself became
for us "righteousness from God and consecration and
redemption" (1 Cor. 1:30). He destroys the enmity in His
flesh and reconciles us to God (cf. Eph. 2:15-16). This
He accomplishes not merely by sharing our nature, nor was
it only when He died for us, but at all times and for every
man. He was crucified then; now He hospitably entertains
us whenever we in penitence ask forgiveness.

He alone, then, was able to render all the honour that
is due to the Father and make satisfaction for that which
had been taken away. The former He achieved by His life,
the latter by His death. The death which He died upon the
cross to the Father's glory He brought in to outweigh the
injury which we had committed; in addition, He most
abundantly made amends for the debt of honour which we
owed for our sins. By His life He paid all honour, both that
which it befitted Him to pay and also that by which the
Father ought to be honoured. Even with the many great works
by which He gave the greatest honour to the Father He also
offered His life which was pure from every sin. He did
this by fulfilling His own laws most exactly and perfectly,
not only those which He Himself observed, for as He says,
"I have kept my Father's commandments" (Jn. 15:10), but
also those which He prescribed for the lives of men. He
alone exemplified and implanted the heavenly philosophy
on earth. This He did also by the very miracles of which
He proclaimed the Father to be the Author (Jn. 14:10).

In addition to all these things, who does not know that
by the very fact that He was among men and thus fully
united with our flesh Christ most clearly and evidently
showed forth the kindness and love for mankind of Him

who sent Him, and thus rendered the glory which was the Father's due? If kindness is to be measured by good deeds, God in His dispensation has so benefited the human race that He has spared nothing, but has included all the riches of His being in human nature for, as it says, "in Him [Christ] dwells the whole fullness of Deity bodily" (Col. 2:9). It is obvious that in the Saviour we have come to know the utmost limit of God's love for man. By the things which He has done He alone taught men how God loves the world and how great is His concern for mankind. By them He led Nicodemus to the knowledge of the Father's love for men. He regards it as a sufficient proof of God's infinite love for the world that "He gave His only Son, that whoever believes in Him should not perish, but have eternal life" (Jn. 3:16).

If, then, the Father had no greater or better graces to give than those which He bestowed on human nature at the descent of His only-begotten Son, it is clear that man could have rendered no glory to God greater than that which the kindness and love that he has received from Him already proclaim. For this reason the Saviour honours the Father through Himself in a manner befitting Himself and Him who has begotten Him. For in what else could the honour of God consist than in being shown to be pre-eminently good?

This is the glory which was His due from of old; yet it was possible for no human being to offer it to Him. Therefore He says, "if I am a father, where is my honour?" (Mal. 1:6). The only-begotten Son alone was able to fulfill all that is the Father's due. This very fact He points out after He has completed His whole work when He says to the Father whom He has honoured, "I glorified Thee on earth, I have manifested Thy name to men" (Jn. 17:4, 6)—and fittingly so. He is the Logos, who bears the express image of Him who begat Him—"He reflects His glory and bears the very stamp of His nature" (Heb. 1:3). Since, by being joined to flesh, He became intelligible to those who lived by sense, He made known the good will of the Mind who had brought Him forth. It is to this, I think, that the saying refers, when the Saviour says to Philip who wishes to see the Father, "he

who has seen Me has seen the Father" (Jn. 14:9). Therefore
Isaiah says, "He shall be called 'Angel of Mighty Counsel' "
(Is. 9:6 LXX).

[§ 5. The Eucharist as the application of the atonement]

Since, therefore, the only-begotten Son has left nothing
undone which pertains to the Father's glory, He alone "breaks
down the dividing wall of hostility" (Eph. 2:14) and clears
man from his indictment. Since Jesus, being of twofold
nature, in accordance with His humanity which He shares
with us honoured the Father and wove for Him that wondrous
crown of glory from His Body and Blood, Christ's Body
then is the only medicine against sin and His Blood the
only ransom from offences.

For this reason He existed at the beginning—that He
should glorify the Father. As the Saviour Himself says, "for
this I was born and for this I came into the world" (Jn.
18:37). In all the time thereafter He did nothing else but
fulfill every work tending to this end; He suffered no pain
but what particularly served this purpose. So His Body became the treasury of the fulness of Deity. He tasted no
sin but fulfilled all righteousness; He proclaimed to His
brothers the Father whom they had not known, both by
what He spoke and through His deeds.

This is the Body that was slain upon the cross and which
underwent the preliminaries of the slaying by suffering
fear and agony and flowing with sweat, by being betrayed,
arrested, and enduring lawless judges. In its "testimony under
Pontius Pilate it made the good confession," as Paul says
(1 Tim. 6:14); it paid the penalty of death for this confession, and that upon the cross. It received lashes upon the
back, nails in the hands and feet, the lance in the side; it
suffered pain by being scourged, and torment by being
nailed. The Blood springing out of the wounds darkened
the sun and shook the earth; it hallowed the air and washed
the whole world clean from the filth of sin.

The written law stood in need of the spiritual law; that which was imperfect needed that which is perfect—being unable to perfect the virtuous, it needed that which was capable thereof. In the same way the sorrow and tears of those who repent of sins after the baptismal washing and entreat for grace stand in need of the Blood of the New Covenant and of the Body which was slain, since they are of no avail without them.

[§ 6. How this Mystery unites us to Christ]

The divine Dionysius* tells us that the divine Mysteries themselves do not sanctify and are incapable of their proper effects without the sacred feast being added to them. How much less is it likely that men's efforts and righteousness should be capable of releasing from sin and achieving the other results! Besides, there is also among the Holy Mysteries that which, when men repent of their sins and confess them to the priests, delivers them from every penalty of God the Judge. Yet even of this Mystery they are not able to obtain the effect unless they feast at the sacred banquet.

For this reason we are baptized but once, but approach the table frequently, for we from time to time offend against God since we are human. But such as seek to cancel the indictment stand in need of penitence, effort, and triumph over sin. Yet this they will not achieve without adding the only remedy against man's sins.

When the wild olive has been grafted on to it, the good olive entirely assimilates it so that its fruit is no longer proper to the wild olive tree. In the same way men's righteousness by itself avails nothing. But once men are united to Christ's Flesh and Blood by partaking of them, straightway the greatest benefits result, the remission of sins and the inheriting of the kingdom, which are the fruits of Christ's righteousness. Just as we receive from the holy table a Body

---

*Eastern mystical writer, highly regarded in the mediaeval West no less than in the Eastern Church, who was often erroneously identified with Dionysius the Areopagite, disciple of St. Paul (Acts 17:34).

far superior to our own, the Body of Christ, so in conse-
quence our righteousness becomes a Christlike righteousness.
The saying, "we are the Body of Christ and individually
members of it" (1 Cor. 12:27) should not be regarded as
referring merely to our body. Far more justly we should
ascribe this participation to the soul and its activity, since
"he who is united to the Lord becomes one spirit with him"
(1 Cor. 6:17). These words show that this participation and
growing together apply particularly to mind and soul.

For this cause He did not merely clothe Himself in a
body,* but He also assumed a soul, mind, and will and
everything else that is human, in order to be united to the
whole of our nature and completely penetrate us and resolve
us into Himself by totally joining what is His to that which
is ours.

Since in respect to sin alone He can have nothing in
common with us, He can have no concord with those who
sin nor be united with them. Out of love for man He
received all other things from us, and out of even greater
love He joins what is His to us. The first means that God
has come down to earth, the second that He has taken us
from earth to heaven. So, on the one hand God became incarnate, on the other man has been deified. In the former
case mankind as a whole is freed from reproach in that
Christ has overcome sin in one body and one soul; in the
latter each man individually is released from sin and made
acceptable to God, which is an even greater act of love for
man. Since it was not possible for us to ascend to Him and
participate in that which is His, He came down to us and
partook of that which is ours. So perfectly has He coalesced
with that which He has taken that He imparts Himself to
us by giving us what He has assumed from us. As we partake
of His human Body and Blood we receive God Himself into
our souls. It is thus God's Body and Blood which we receive,
His soul, mind, and will, no less than those of His humanity.

---

*The Apollinarian error, which ascribes to Christ an incomplete human
nature, and which was formally condemned by the Council of Constantinople
in 381.

It was necessary that the remedy for my weakness be God and become man, for were He God only He would not be united to us, for how could He become our feast? On the other hand, if Christ were no more than what we are, his feast would have been ineffectual. Now, however, since He is both at once, He is united to those who have the same nature as Himself and coalesces with us men. By His divinity He is able to exalt and transcend our human nature and to transform it into Himself. For when the greater powers are brought to bear upon the lesser they do not permit them to retain their own characteristics; when iron comes together with fire it retains nothing of the property of iron, when earth and water are thrown on fire they exchange their properties for those of fire. If, then, of those which have similar powers the stronger thus affect the weaker, what must we think of His wonderfully great power?

It is clear, then, that Christ infuses Himself into us and mingles Himself with us. He changes and transforms us into Himself, as a small drop of water is changed by being poured into an immense sea of ointment. This ointment can do such great things to those who fall into it, that it not only makes us to be sweet-smelling and redolent thereof, but our whole state becomes the sweet-smelling savour of the perfume which was poured out for us as it says, "for we are the sweet savour of Christ" (2 Cor. 2:15).

[§ 7. How Christ's flesh sets us free from the law of the flesh]

Great is the power and the grace of the feast for its communicants, if we approach it pure from all wickedness and introduce no evil afterwards. If we are prepared, nothing prevents Christ from being perfectly united to us. "This is a great mystery" said blessed Paul (Eph. 5:32), referring to this union. This is the celebrated marriage by which the most holy Bridegroom espouses the Church as His Bride. It is here that Christ feeds the choir that surrounds Him; by this Mystery alone we become "flesh of His flesh, and bone

of His bones" (Gen. 2:21). These are the terms in which
the apostle describes the marriage. John [the Baptist], speaking as the friend of the Bridegroom (Jn. 3:28), points out
Christ as the Bridegroom and as possessing the Bride.

This Mystery is the light for those who have already
been cleansed. It is a means of cleansing for those who are
undergoing cleansing, it is the anointing of those who enter
the contest against evil passions. Those who have been
cleansed have nothing more to do than to receive the light
of the world, like an eye that has rid itself of dirt. As for
those who are still in need of that which can cleanse them,
what other means of cleansing have they? For "the blood
of the Son of God cleanses us from all sin" (Jn. 1:7), as
John says, who is particularly beloved of Christ. As for the
victory over the evil one, who does not know that Christ
alone has won it and set up His Body as the only trophy of
victory over sin? By this Body He is able to succour those
who are under attack; in it He Himself suffered and overcame when He was tempted (cf. Heb. 2:18).

Since our flesh had nothing in common with the spiritual
life, but was at enmity with it and exceedingly hostile towards it—as it is said, "its desires are against the Spirit" (Gal.
5:17)—therefore a flesh was devised against that flesh
which is earthly, the spiritual flesh. By a law of flesh the
carnal law is abrogated, and flesh yields to spirit and aids
it against the law of sin. For this reason it was possible for
no one at all to live the spiritual life before this blessed
flesh had come into being. The very law itself was not being
kept, though it had not yet been greatly complicated by
philosophy. Nor was there anything among men which had
power to help us against our innate misfortune. For, as it
is said, the law "was weakened by the flesh" (Rom. 8:3), and
it stood in need of another flesh which was able to preserve
its power. "For God," Paul says, "has done what the law,
weakened by the flesh, could not do, sending His own Son
in the likeness of sinful flesh He condemned sin in the flesh"
(ibid.).

For these reasons we are always in need of this divine
flesh and constantly partake of the table, so that the law

of the Spirit might be active in us and that there be no place left for the life of the flesh, nor any opportunity to fall back to the earth, like heavy bodies when the support is withdrawn. For the Mystery is perfect for all purposes, and its partakers stand in need of nothing which it does not supply in a most excellent way.

[§ 8. How the Eucharist enables us to worship "in spirit and in truth"]

Yet we are such wretched material that the seal cannot remain unaffected, "for we have this treasure in earthen vessels" (2 Cor. 4:7). We therefore partake of the remedy, not once for all, but constantly. The potter must constantly sit by the clay and repeatedly restore the shape which is being blurred. We must continually experience the Physician's hand as He heals the decaying matter and raises up the failing will, lest death creep in unawares. For it says, "even when we were dead through trespasses He made us alive together with Christ" (Eph. 2:5), and "the blood of Christ shall purify your conscience from dead works to serve the living God" (Heb. 9:14). The power of the holy table draws to us the true life from that blessed Heart, and there we become able to worship God purely.

If, then, the pure worship of God consists in being subject to Him, obeying Him, doing all things as He moves us, I know not how we are capable of being subject to God more than by becoming His members. Who, more than the head, can command the members of the body? While every other sacred rite makes its recipients into members of Christ, the Bread of Life effects this most perfectly. For, as the members live because of the head and the heart, so, He says, "he who eats me will live because of me" (Jn. 6:57).

So also man lives because of food, but not in the same way in this sacred rite. Since natural food is not itself living it does not of itself infuse life into us, but by aiding the life which is in the body it appears to those who eat to be the cause of life. But the Bread of Life is Himself living,

and through Him those to whom He imparts Himself
truly live. While natural food is changed into him who feeds
on it, and fish and bread and any other kind of food become
human blood, here it is entirely opposite. The Bread of Life
Himself changes him who feeds on Him and transforms
and assimilates him into Himself. As He is the Head and
the Heart, we depend on Him for moving and living since
He possesses life.

This the Saviour Himself reveals. He does not sustain
our life in the same way as food; but since He Himself has
life by nature He breathes it into us, just as the heart or the
head imparts life to the members. So He calls Himself "the
living Bread" (Jn. 6:51) and says, "he who eats me will
live because of me" (Jn. 6:57).

It appears therefore, that to "worship God in spirit and
in truth" (Jn. 4:24) and to offer Him pure homage is an
effect of the holy table. From this Mystery therefore we
obtain the gift of being Christ's members and thus of being
like Him. While we were dead it was impossible to offer
homage to the living God. But unless we constantly feast at
the banquet it is impossible to be alive and to be released
from dead works. Just as "God is spirit, and those who
worship Him must worship in spirit and in truth" (Jn. 4:24),
so it is fitting that those who choose to worship the Living
One should themselves be living, for, as He says, "He is
not God of the dead, but of the living" (Mt. 22:32).

[§ 9. How the Eucharist makes us sons of God]

Thus to live according to right reason and to tend towards
virtue is to worship God. The former might be the work of
slaves too, for He says, "when you have done all these
things, say 'we are unworthy servants' " (Lk. 17:10). But
this worship can only come from sons. It is not, then, to the
rank of slaves, but of sons, that we are called. For this
reason we share His Flesh and Blood, as it says, "the
children share in flesh and blood" (Heb. 2:14). As He
became a partaker with us of flesh and blood in order that

He might become our Father and be able to utter His word, "Behold I and the children which God has given me" (Is. 8:18), so must we partake of His Flesh and Blood that we might become His sons. In this way through the sacred rite we become not merely His members, but also His sons, in order that we may worship Him with willing subjection and with a ready mind. This worship is so wonderful and marvellous that it must be described by the simile of both sons and members, since neither by itself suffices to describe the reality. In the case of the one, is it strange that we have no proper motion of our own but are moved by God, just as our members are moved by the head? In the other case, is it surprising that even as we are subject to our fleshly fathers, so we should be subject to the Father of spirits (Heb. 12:9)? But that we should be able at the same time to be subject as members and yet retain the autonomy of reason is indeed a wondrous thing!

This is the reality of our adoption as sons of God. Unlike human adoptions, it does not consist in the mere name, nor does it confer honour merely to the extent that those who have been adopted share the name of those who have been naturally born and have the same father as they, without having undergone the same birth and its pangs. In this case, however, there is a real birth and a sharing with the only-begotten Son, not of the surname only, but of His very Being, His Blood, His Body, His Life. What, then, is greater than that the Father of the only-begotten Son Himself recognizes in us His members and finds the very form of the Son in our faces? It says, "He predestined them to be conformed to the image of His Son" (Rom. 8:29).

Why then should I call this sonship fictitious, when it makes us more alike in nature and more closely akin than natural sonship? Those who are thus generated are sons of God more than those who are naturally born, and that to the same extent as genuine sons are more truly sons than those who are adopted. What is it that makes men our true fathers? It is the fact that our flesh is derived from theirs, and our life is produced from their blood. This applies to the Saviour as well. We are flesh from His flesh and bones

from His bones. Yet there is a considerable difference between these two participations. In the case of the natural
sons their blood no longer belongs to their parents, though
it was theirs before it became that of the sons. So kinship
arises from the fact that what once belonged to the parents
now belongs to the offspring. But the effect of the sacred
rite is that the blood by which we live is even now Christ's
Blood, and the flesh by which the Mystery establishes us is
Christ's Body, and further, that we have members and life
in common with Him.

True communion consists in this: that the same thing is
present simultaneously to both parties. When, however, both
parties have it, the one at one time, the other at another
time, it is not so much a sharing as a separation. There is
no joining together since that which one alone possesses is
not present with both parties in the same way. Thus they
neither share with each other nor have they anything really
in common. In other words, when something belongs to one
party at one time and to another at another time, it is merely
a semblance of sharing. One does not live with a person
merely by living in the same house after he has left, nor
has one a share in the office and business and cares of a
person merely by succeeding to his office. Just as only he
who lives in the same house or occupies the same office at
the same time shares it with another person, so it is in this
case. Since we do not possess them at the same time as our
parents we do not share their flesh and blood. But with
Christ we truly share, since we at all times possess body,
blood, members, and suchlike in common with Him.

If then sharing in flesh and blood makes us sons, it is
clear that the table has made us more closely akin to the
Saviour than birth has made us akin to our very parents.
Unlike them He has not been parted from us once He has
given us life, but He is with us at all times and united to us.
By His presence He gives us life and sustains us in being.
Nothing prevents those who are separated from their parents
from surviving them; for those who are separated from
Christ there remains nothing but to die. And why do I not
speak of that which is greater? For [natural] sons it is im-

possible to be thus unless they are separated from those who beget them. The very fact of initial separation [in this case] causes some to beget and others to be begotten. In the case of the Mysteries, however, sonship consists in being united and sharing, while separation means perishing and no longer existing.

[§ 10. How the Eucharist forms the new man in Christ]

If, therefore, the name of kinship signifies some kind of sharing and, as I think, indicates those who share in common blood, then the only sharing of blood, the only kinship and sonship, is that which we share with Christ. Accordingly, when men have received this kind of birth it conceals even their natural generation, for it says, "as many as received him, he gave them power to become children of God" (Jn. 1:12). Even though they have already been begotten, and those who begat them were flesh, and natural generation preceded the spiritual, yet the second birth so greatly prevails over the first that neither trace nor name of it remains. Thus, as the Holy Bread brings in the new man, it uproots and casts out the old. This too is an effect of the holy table, for it says that "those who received him were not born of blood" (Jn. 1:13). Whenever we receive Him we experience this word "Receive" (Mt. 26:26) and the Mystery of which it was spoken. It is clear that we are called to the banquet in which we truly take Christ into our hands and receive Him with our mouth, in which we are mingled with Him in soul and united to Him in body and commingled in blood. And rightly so; for those who receive the Saviour and hold on to Him to the end He is Himself the Head which governs and they are members fit for Him.

It follows, then, that the members should undergo the same birth as the Head. That Flesh did not take its origin "from blood, nor from the will of flesh, nor of the will of a man, but from God" (Jn. 1:13), from the Holy Spirit, for "that which was conceived in her is of the Holy Spirit"

(Mt. 1:20). It was fitting that the members also should be
born in this way, since this birth of the Head was the birth
of the blessed members; for it was the birth of the Head
which brought the members into existence. If, then, birth is
the beginning of life for a person, so that to be born is to
begin one's life, and Christ is the life of those who cleave
to Him, then they were born when Christ entered this life
and was born into it.

So great, then, is the abundance of benefits from the holy
table. It delivers from judgment; it wipes out the disgrace
which comes from sin. It renews our youth; it binds us
closer to Christ Himself than any physical bonds. In short,
of all sacred rites the Eucharist eminently perfects us in true
Christianity.

[§ 11. The Eucharist compared with Baptism

a) With regard to the purification bestowed]

For many it is a cause for amazement, that while this
Mystery is thus the most perfect of all, and greater than
Baptism, it yet seems to avail less for release from guilt.
Baptism does so without any preceding effort, while the
Eucharist requires effort on our part. As for those who have
been cleansed in Baptism, there is no difference between
them and those who have not begun to incur any defilement
whatever, while many of those who frequent the banquet
bear traces of the sins which they have committed.

Let us make the distinction clearer. In the case of sins
committed we notice these four things—the one who has
committed sin, the evil action itself, the penalty incurred
thereby, the consequent evil inclination which has been
intruded into the soul. He who has committed sin must of
himself break with the action, and when he has ceased from
it he must come to the baptismal washing. The other things,
both the guilt and the disease, Baptism straightway removes
without any further effort. Thus we believe that it somehow
slays the very man who has sinned, for he dies in the waters,

and it is a new man whom the washing restores to us.

When one receives the Holy Bread, after such affliction and pains as befit our sinful condition, it releases him from guilt and purifies the soul from its evil state. In nowise, however, does it slay, since it does not avail to create anew. Him who will not amend his life it leaves behind and permits to remain within the bounds of sin, not merely because he is guilty, but because he is presumptuous. There are also those who still bear the signs of sickness and the scars of old wounds because they are not as concerned about their wounds as they ought to be and come without sufficient preparation of soul for the power of the remedy.

So this Mystery differs from Baptism in respect of purification in that it is not spoken of as putting to death him who has sinned and creating him anew, but as merely cleansing him while he still remains himself, and that not without effort on his part. The guilty is cleansed in Baptism by being washed, but in the Eucharist by being fed.

[b) With regard to the co-operation required of us]

This I will say concerning the effort required of us. Since Baptism receives those who have not yet been united nor have received any strength for running the race for goodness, it fittingly achieves all things for us by a free gift. It has need of nothing on our part—as though we could contribute anything to it. The table, however, is set forth for those who already have been united and who are alive and are able to fend for themselves. It enables us to use the power and the weapons which have been given us and to pursue goodness, no longer as though we were being carried or dragged along, but spontaneously bestirring ourselves and moving as already skilled runners.

Why was it necessary to cause us to receive that which we were not compelled to use? What would be the point of strengthening and arming him who was to remain and sleep at home? Were there not a time for struggle and effort on the part of those who either had been born at the beginning or were subsequently willing to be cleansed, I know not when we should become useful even to ourselves. Were there no contests for virtue, what would be man's work? Or rather, what would be worse than the case of those who achieve nothing whatever that is worthy of praise, but instead keep the soul busied with evil at all times?

It was therefore necessary to grant to men a place for works and a time for struggles, and to give to those who had already received perfection and ability from the Mysteries an opportunity to make the effort befitting their nature. When the day appears "which the Lord has made" (Ps. 118:24) we should no longer be asleep but occupied in deeds as David says: "man goes forth to his work and to his labour until the evening" (Ps. 104:23). Just as the night in which no one can work (Jn. 9:4) follows on this day so also before this day there was a night in which it was completely impossible to work. No one knew whither to walk, since that night prevailed on the earth in which, as Christ said, "he who walks does not know where he goes" (Jn. 12:35).

Now that the Sun has risen and diffused His light everywhere by means of the Mysteries there must be no delay of human works and effort. We must feed on our Bread "in the sweat of our face" (Gen. 3:19) since it is "broken for us" (1 Cor. 11:24), for it is appointed only for those who are endowed with reason. Since it is the Lord who says, "Labour for the food which endures" (Jn. 6:27), He commands us not to be idle and inactive, but to come to His banquet as those who are working. If, then, Paul's injunction bans the lazy even from the transitory table of this life, saying, "if anyone is idle, let him not even eat" (2 Thess. 3:10), what works are needed on the part of those who are called to this table!

From what has been said it is clear how we must prepare ourselves to touch the sacred Gifts, and that we must indeed cleanse ourselves of our own accord before the sacred rite. That this is a Mystery not inferior to the others, but even more efficacious, will be clear from the following.

First, if God bestows the greater gifts on those who are superior, it is because He has weighed mercy as in a balance and, according to the prophet, does all things with righteousness as the plummet (Is. 28:17). On those who have been initiated and already have been striving for virtue He bestows far greater benefits than on such as have not yet been baptized. So the latter grace is superior to the former, and those who have been initiated obtain yet better gifts. The former is Baptism, the latter is the sacred banquet which is rightly considered to be so much more perfect since there is need of greater preparation on the part of those who approach it. It would not be reasonable were the greater gift available to all who desired it, while the lesser were available only to those who have been cleansed by their struggles or by the Mysteries. On the contrary, it is reasonable to conclude that the latter gift is more perfect, since it is not obtained save by many and noble efforts.

[§ 12. Christ as our Ally in the struggle]

This also we must consider, that Christ who is our Host at His feast fights at our side. But one who fights at our side comes to the aid not of those who are slothful or inactive through sickness, but to those who are fit and strong and courageous and who fight nobly and bravely against the foe.

So Christ, as He acts in each of His Mysteries, becomes all things to us, our Creator as He washes us in Baptism, the one who anoints for the contest in the holy chrism, our Ally as He feeds us in the Eucharist. So He creates the members at the beginning and then strengthens them with the Spirit. On the table He is actually present and endures the contest with us to the very end. After our departure He will award the prizes, and for His Saints He will sit as the Judge of the labours in which He has shared. At the triumph, when the victors are to be crowned, He Himself is their crown.

So when He creates and anoints us, He supplies all that is needed for boldness and perseverance in the contests which are on behalf of philosophy. When He fights at our side

He does not supply everything; at the time of triumph He supplies nothing. It is not reasonable that He who anoints and He who creates should leave anything undone that is capable of preparing the athlete for the contest, nor that the fellow Athlete should take on Himself the whole responsibility for His comrade and allow him to take his ease while He alone strips for the contest. Nor is it fitting that the umpire or the crown should anoint or train or perform the offices of a physician, nor to ascribe to the athlete another's victory, courage, strength, or any other excellence, but only to ascertain and reward the victory which is obviously his own.

For those who have excelled it is better to be crowned than merely to win the contest. To be winners is better than merely to be trained, for the training is for the sake of winning, and victory for the sake of the crowns. But if it is taken as a sign of imperfection and inferiority that this Mystery does not in every way prepare or create, then the ultimate of blessedness would be too weak to confer happiness on men. But our blessedness is to receive God who crowns us, to partake of Him at the table under the veils, which is greater than if the table were to confer some preparation and cleansing and none of these crowns. One ought not then to marvel that while the banquet is more perfect a Mystery, yet it avails less for cleansing.

In addition to what we have said, this gift is also a prize. A reward does not produce or make champions, but rather it indicates and adorns them. So in the banquet Christ not only cleanses us and fights at our side, He is also the prize which those who have contended are to receive. What else is there for the blessed ones in recompense for their efforts here than to receive Christ and to be with Him? When Paul had run that course he said that departure hence issues in the final rest with Christ, for he says, "my desire is to depart and be with Christ, for that is far better" (Phil. 1:23).

It is this which is the supreme effect of the banquet. Even though Christ may be found with the other Mysteries as well, yet we receive them in preparation for being with Him at His banquet where we receive Him unalloyed. To which of the others does it pertain that we become one body and one spirit with Him, and that we abide in Him, and He abides in us? This is I think why Christ Himself speaks of the blessedness of the righteous as of a banquet at which He Himself waits upon them (Lk. 12:37).

[§ 13. How, in the Eucharist, Christ is the reward for victory]

It is in this way, then, that the Bread of Life is a prize. Those who receive this gift are still walking and travelling on the earth, and so are covered with dust, stumble on the way, and are in fear of falling into the hands of brigands. Yet the gift amply suffices for their present needs. It supplies them with strength, it guides them, it cleanses them, until they find lodging in that place where, according to Peter's word, it is good for a man to be (Mt. 17:4). In that place there is no room for other things, and men abide where they are free from worldly affairs. Christ alone is their crown and is clearly present with them.

Since, then, the Eucharist is a means of purification and ordained as such from the beginning, it frees us from all defilement. Christ, who takes part with us in those contests in which He was the Leader and the first who stripped Himself for action, supplies us with strength against those who war against us. Because He is also the reward implies no lack of effort on our part. If, then, one holds that the banquet is the reward and the final blessedness, what sense does it make to pretend that it is of little avail?

It is not because it lacks great power that the Eucharist fails to reshape him who has been corrupted by sin, but rather because he is unable to receive and experience it. As we have said above, the one who is baptized already possesses the primal form which even the uttermost wickedness cannot obliterate from his soul. It is impossible to be removed, even if he has the audacity to deny his acknowledged and bounden service to the Lord of all, since neither the highest philosophy nor the mere act of confession was capable of imprinting this image in the first place.

Since, then, the man is altogether beyond dying and wasting away (which a new creation pre-supposes), he cannot be created afresh. The death applies to the old image of carnal man, and it is this which is capable of dying, for as John [the Baptist] says, "the axe is laid to the root of the trees" (Mt. 3:10). But he who has been baptized already wears the new man. How then shall he die who is joined to that Adam who "dies no more" (Rom. 6:9)? And for what reason should he die, who had to die in order to receive Christ whom he still bears in his soul?

Another regeneration would be impossible and unnecessary by reason of the very reception of the baptismal washing. How should the one rite be greater than the other by reason of that which can be found in neither? Not even Baptism itself is capable of regenerating anew those who have undergone it and been formed by it, and the sacred ordinance therefore never washed any man twice. This is not merely because a certain pattern or order is observed, but because it is impossible for anyone to be born twice in the same way.

[§ 14. Excursus—a comparison of martyrdom and Baptism]

Yet someone will object that to die confessing the [Christian] religion against persecutors is a Baptism. Why then have many who had undergone initiation in water run this race? Did they by this means receive a second baptismal washing?

The answer which we must give to this question is that those who have chosen to be united to Christ and to live with Him are commended both by the fact that they were formed by His hand in the good form, and also because they arrived at the goal on their own by virtue and by the contests [i.e., martyrdom] which are worthy of praise. So Baptism in water forms the man and avails for this alone, but death for Christ clearly has the twofold virtue of supplying that which the water supplies and also that which must be contributed by us.

For those, then, who have not yet been initiated there is a Baptism and a forming as they bear witness to Christ and are buried with Him, in which the essence of Baptism consists. There is also their virtue, which is full of toil for goodness and of final perseverance.

Now for those who have been initiated, the first result does not apply since they have already been created and are alive. The second aspect remains, for it consists in the exercise of godliness and the achievement of virtue and of the knowledge of Christ and of love for Him above all that can be loved, and in holding nothing more firmly than trust in Him. Of these sword and fire and extreme torments are a sure and tested proof.

For these reasons it is by no means lawful for those who have once been initiated by Baptism to undergo it a second time, since it is incapable of conferring anything beyond that which we have already received and possess therefrom. To undergo martyrdom is most certainly lawful, since it is able not only to give new birth and to form, but also to prepare crowns for noble deeds. By it both are conferred on those who have not yet been initiated, the latter only on those who have. It is nothing novel, then, that since martyrdom brings perfection in both ways, those who have no need of the one should obtain the other which they need. Similarly, since the Gifts of the holy table have the power to cleanse those who have not yet received them, they are able to enlighten those who already have been cleansed. Nothing, then, prevents those who have obtained the one gift from drawing near to the Mystery for the sake of the other. Of these things enough has been said!

[§ 15. The sanctifying effects of the Eucharist]

It is the sacred banquet, then, which has led us to discuss whether the perfect communion with God which it effects ought to be called worship, or adoption of sons, or both. It makes us more akin to Christ than birth makes us akin to our parents, since it is not a foundation of insignificant particles of His Body and of small drops of His Blood that it provides us, but it imparts them in their perfection. It is not, like our parents, the cause of life, but life itself. Nor is it called life because it causes life in the way that He called His apostles light because they were appointed as our guides to the light (Mt. 5:14), but because by Him we are truly able to live, since He is the very life itself.

Since He makes those who cleave to Him holy and righteous, He not only instructs them and teaches them what is necessary and leads the soul to virtue and its faculty of right reasoning into action, but also He Himself becomes for them "righteousness from God and sanctification" (1 Cor. 1:30).

In this way the saints are holy and blessed because of the Blessed One who is with them. Through Him they become alive instead of dead, wise instead of unwise, holy, righteous, and sons of God instead of polluted, wicked, and slaves. From themselves and from human nature and effort there is nothing whatever which enables them to be justly so called. Rather, they are holy because of the Holy One, righteous and wise because of the righteous and wise One who abides with them. In short, if any men are really worthy of being called by these great and august names, their appellation derives from Him, especially because their own efforts and powers are so far from capable of making them righteous and wise that their righteousness is mere wickedness, their wisdom sheer folly.

In addition, even if virtue has made us most honourable and has adorned us with the names which are proper to the righteousness and wisdom which pertain to God, rather than to that derived from man and attained by our own zeal, we may fitly attribute them to the latter rather than to the former. It is not by the names of things which are external and alien to us that we are called, but of those which are our own and which are inherent to our nature. It is not our dwelling or clothing which dispose us to one character or the other, or which give us the name of vice or virtue, but those of our characteristics which are especially our own which affect us and entitle us to be called accordingly. The things of Christ, however, are ours more than our very selves. They belong to us because we have become His members, His sons, and share flesh and blood and spirit with Him. They are closer to us not only than that which comes by training, but even closer than that which is the result of our nature since, as has been shown, He is more akin to us than our very parents.

For these reasons we are obliged, not to introduce mere human philosophy or contend for its rewards, but to live the new life in Christ and to display its righteousness. This would not be possible unless we had a special fitness for it and unless it were especially suitable for us. For this cause then "we were buried with him by baptism, that we might walk in newness of life" (Rom. 6:4). To Timothy Paul says, "take hold of eternal life" (1 Tim. 6:12). So also it is said, "be holy as he who called you is holy" (1 Pet. 1:15, Lev. 19:2), and "be merciful," not with human mercy but "as your Father is merciful" (Lk. 6:36), and "love one another even as I have loved you" (Jn. 13:34). With this love Paul "yearned with the affection of Christ Jesus" (Phil. 1:8). Wherefore the Saviour Himself enjoined the disciples to be at peace and infused into them His very own peace—"my peace I give to you" (Jn. 14:26)—and prayed to the Father "that the love with which thou hast loved me may be in them" (Jn. 17:26).

[§ 16. How this union with Christ delivers from sin]

In short, just as the new birth is one which is divine and supernatural, so also the new life and its mode and philosophy and all things are new and spiritual. This the Saviour declares when He says to Nicodemus, "that which is born of the Spirit is spirit" (Jn. 3:6). Hence Paul also says, "that I may be found in him not having a righteousness of my own, based on law, but that which is through faith in Christ, the righteousness of God" (Phil. 3:9).

This righteousness is the royal robe, for what is ours

is proper to slaves. But how could freedom and kingship, towards which we must hasten, belong to slaves? As for those who display no more than the virtue of slaves, how could they appear worthy of a kingdom? For just as "the perishable does not inherit the imperishable," but "this perishable nature must put on the imperishable, and this mortal nature must put on immortality" (1 Cor. 15:50, 53), in the same manner our slavish works will not suffice us for the kingdom. It will require the righteousness which is from God. For the heir must be a son, not a slave, for "the slave," He says, "does not continue in the house for ever, the Son continues for ever" (Jn. 8:35).

Therefore every one who is to attain to that lot must first cast off the state of a slave and exhibit that of a son. This means that we must come with the features of the only-begotten Son on our faces and appear before the Father with His beauty. This means that we are set free from all slavery by the Son of God, as Christ says to the Jews, "If the Son sets you free, you will be free indeed" (Jn. 8:36). He, then, sets the slaves free and makes them sons of God, since He Himself is the Son of God and free from every sin. He makes them to share in His body, blood, spirit, and everything that is His. It is in this way that He both re-created us and set us free and deified us as He, the healthful, free, and true God mingled Himself with us.

Thus the sacred banquet makes Christ, who is our true righteousness, to be our good, greater than our own natural good things. So we glory in His good gifts and are distinguished for them as though we had succeeded on our own, and even bear their name if only we preserve our sharing in them. So if anyone who is truly holy and righteous hears of any good quality for which he has gained credit, it is from Christ that he has received it. For it is said, "my soul shall make her boast in the Lord" (Ps. 34:3), and "in Him shall all nations be blessed" (Gen. 12:3).

Hence we demand nothing merely human, but the things of Christ, that we may bring them into our souls and with them depart this life. Thus we shall in every way display this philosophy and this new wealth before receiving any crowns, without introducing any of the false coin, since this is the only tribute which is useful for the kingdom which is in heaven.

Since, then, the prize which we must strive to obtain is God Himself, it is necessary that there be someone which is proportionate to the prize and that the contests be divine. God must be not only the anointer of the athletes and the one who presides over the contests, but He Himself must also be the one who succeeds in them, so that the end corresponds to the preparation and the preparation to the end which is sought. When He put us on earth He did nothing and required from us nothing that was beyond our nature. So as He leads us to God and sets us free from earth He has permitted us to retain nothing that is merely human, but He adapted Himself to all the things of which we were in need, and left nothing undone of the things which could prepare us for that goal.

[§ 17. How Christ re-creates us through the Eucharist]

If, then, one speaks of our condition as a disease in need of a cure, Christ did not merely go to the patient and deign to look at him and touch him, but with His own hand wrought what was needed for healing, and even became Himself our medicine and diet and whatever else is conducive to health. Or, if we speak of a re-creation, it is from Himself and from His own flesh that He restored what is necessary, and He substituted Himself for that which had been destroyed. It was not from the same matter as that which He first created that He created afresh. Then He made man out of dust taken from the earth (Gen. 2:7), but when He created him the second time He gave His own Body. As He restores his life he does not improve the soul, since it remains in its natural state, but as He pours His Blood into the hearts of those who have been initiated He makes His own life to dawn upon them. At the beginning it says that "He breathed into him the breath of life" (Gen. 2:7), but now He communicates His Spirit to us (Jn. 20:22) for it says, "God has sent the Spirit of His Son into our hearts, crying 'Abba! Father!' " (Gal. 4:6). Since there was need of light at the beginning, He said, "Let there be light," and there was light (Gen. 1:3). That light was a subservient one; but now the Master Himself, as Paul says, "has shone in our hearts, He who said, 'Let light shine out of darkness' " (2 Cor. 4:6).

In sum—at the beginning God conferred benefits on our race by means of visible creatures and guided man by commands, emissaries, and laws, partly through angels, partly through holy men. Now He uses Himself without intermediary, and acts through Himself for all purposes.

Let us take a fresh look at the matter. He did not send an angel to save the human race, but came in person. It was necessary for men to learn the purposes of His coming. So He did not stay in His own place and send for those who were to hear, but He Himself went about and sought out those to whom He would impart His words. Bringing on His tongue the greatest benefits, He came to the doors of those who stood in need of health. Thus He healed the sick by coming to them Himself and touching them with His hand. He created eyes for him who was born blind by putting clay on his face, having Himself made it by spitting on the ground and kneading it with His finger and taking it up (Jn. 9:6). It says that "He came and touched the bier" (Lk. 7:14), and that He stood by the tomb of Lazarus (Jn. 11:38) and uttered His voice nearby. Although, had He so willed, He might have achieved both these things, and even things in every way greater than these, by mere word and gesture from afar, yet He did it in this way. The latter was an evident sign of His power, while the former was a sign of His love which He came to show towards men.

[§ 18. How Christ by setting us free becomes our King]

Further, when it was necessary that the captives of Hades be set free, He did not entrust this work to angels or

archangels, but He Himself descended into that prison. Since
it was fitting that the captives should not receive freedom
gratuitously, but by being ransomed, He set them free by
shedding His Blood. It is in this way that from thenceforth
to the last day He sets us free and remits punishment and
washes souls from defilement.

He Himself is the means by which He cleanses, as Paul
points out saying, "when through Himself He had made
purification for sins, He sat down at the right hand of the
throne of the majesty on high" (Heb. 1:3). For this reason
Paul calls Christ a servant and himself one who ministers
to Him (Rom. 15:8, 16), and states that He was sent into the
world by the Father to be a servant (cf. Phil. 2:7, Mt. 20:28).

Above all, it was not in this present life only—when
He appeared and came in human weakness "not that He
might judge the world" (Jn. 3:17)—that He displayed what
pertains to servants and hid all things which pertain to the
Master. Even in the life to come, when He shall come with
power and appear with the glory of the Father to manifest
it and the very kingdom itself, "He will gird Himself," it is
said, "and have them sit at table, and He will come and
serve them" (Lk. 12:37). And rightly so—He "through
whom kings reign and rulers govern the earth" (Prov.
8:15, 16).

In this way He entered upon a pure and genuine kingship,
being sufficient in Himself for kingship. Thus He exercises
leadership over those whom He rules, being more cheerful
towards them than friends yet more exacting than a tyrant,
more tender than a father, more united to them than members of the same body, more necessary than a heart, making
them yield without fear, nor bribing them by rewards, but
by being Himself the power that governs and attaches His
subjects to Himself. For to rule by fear or to make subject
by rewards is not truly to rule, but such obedience must be
regarded as motivated by expectation or threats. Just as He
would not properly rule whose sovereignty was derived elsewhere, so we do not truly serve God if we are subject to
Him in either of these two ways.

Since it was necessary for Him to be king by exercising

the most genuine rule (for it would not befit Him to rule in any other way), He devised the means by which He might achieve this. It was the most unexpected means, for He made use of things which were contrary to His state. In order that He might be the true Master He received the nature of a slave and served the slaves as far as the cross and death. Thus He obtained the souls of the slaves and gained direct control over their wills. For this reason Paul, knowing that this service is the cause of His kingship, says, "He humbled Himself, and became obedient unto death, even death on a cross; therefore God has highly exalted Him" (Phil. 2:8-9). The wonderful Isaiah says, "Therefore He will inherit the portion of many, and divide the spoil of the strong; because His soul was given over to death and He was numbered with the transgressors" (53:12 LXX).

On account of the first creation Christ is Master of our nature, but because of the new creation He gained power over our will. This is truly to rule over men as king, since He has bound and subjected to Himself the authority of reason and the freedom of the will which make man what he is. Of this He also says, "all authority in heaven and earth has been given to me" (Mt. 28:18), as though He who was Master of the world before the ages underwent something new. Indeed, David's saying, "God reigns over the nations" (Ps. 47:8) hints at that kingdom in which "the Gentiles," as Paul says, "are members of the same body, and partakers" (Eph. 3:6) with the Saviour. For in that He is altogether united with our bodies and souls He has become the Master, not of bodies only, but also of souls and wills. He holds sway over the truly self-sufficient and genuine kingdom, Himself governing it by means of Himself just as the soul governs the body and the head its members.

It is those who have decided to love this yoke who are led by Him, as though they were not to live by their own reason nor use their own free will, for it says, "I was like a beast toward thee" (Ps. 73:22). This means that one "hates his own soul and loses it" (Jn. 12:25), and by losing it saves it, when the new creation so prevails that the new

Adam entirely hides the old one, and nothing is left of "the old leaven" (1 Cor. 5:7), nor of its origin, its life, or its end.

[§ 19. How our very bodies benefit from the new life]

Now then, in the case of the old Adam the body was formed from the earth, but the new Adam, it is said, was born of God (cf. Jn. 1:13). Each life has its own proper table which bears witness to it. Earthly nourishment pertains to the former life, while the heavenly table feeds the new man with its own proper food. Therefore, when they come to an earthly end, the one life goes back to the earth from whence it came forth, while the other goes to Christ from whom it was taken.

Each life, then, attains to its end which corresponds to the beginning from which it was brought into being. "As was the man of dust," it says, "so are those who are of the dust; and as is the man of heaven, so are those who are of heaven" (1 Cor. 15:48), not merely because of the soul, but because of the body. It too is heavenly, just as the other life is of the earth with regard to both body and soul. The soul indwells, as it were, the hands of him that is heavenly, and the body is his member. It does not partake of soul, but is filled with the living spirit. After the end of the physical life the soul is alive with a life that is unspeakably beautiful, since it has not truly died at all. As Solomon says, "they seemed to die" (Wis. 3:2), yet not to the wise, but rather "in the sight of the unwise." For just as "Christ being raised from the dead dies no more, death has no longer dominion over Him" (Rom. 6:9), so the members of Christ will not ever see death. How shall they taste death when they are always dependent on the living Heart?

If that which is seen is dust and no more, it is no cause for wonder, for the riches are within. "For your life," it is said, "is hid" (Col. 3:3), and the treasury is an earthen vessel as Paul wrote: "we have this treasure in earthen vessels" (1 Cor. 4:7). To those, then, to whom externals only are apparent, it is merely the clay which is visible.

But when Christ appears this very dust will exhibit its proper beauty. When it appears as a member of that lightning (cf. Lk. 17:24) it will be like the sun and emit the same ray, for He says, "the righteous will shine like the sun in the kingdom of the Father" (Mt. 13:43). That radiance with which Christ was seen by the apostles as shining (cf. Mt. 17:2) He calls 'the kingdom of the Father.' It is the very kingdom of God, as He Himself says, which comes in power to those who have seen Him. On that day the righteous will shine with one brightness and glory. They will become bright by receiving that light, He by imparting it. For this bread, this Body, for which men in this life come to the table in order that they may bring it therefrom, is that which will then appear to all eyes upon the clouds (cf. Mt. 24:30) and in one instant of time will display its splendour to the east and to the west like lightning.

[§ 20. The future glory of those who live in Christ]

With this radiance the blessed ones live, and at death the light does not depart from them. The righteous constantly have light, and they come to that new life shining with it. At the time of universal judgment they will run to Him with whom they will have been all the time. It will then happen that for each of those who rise to life the wholeness of the body will be preserved as its bones and parts and members come together with its head. And so it will happen to the common Head of all, Christ the Saviour.

So when He flashes like lightning upon the clouds He will receive His own members from all places, as God in the midst of gods, the glorious Leader of the glorious company. Just as bodies suspended in the air move to earth as soon as their bonds are broken and immediately seek the centre of the earth, so also the bodies of the saints are fixed to the earth because they are bound and continue to be tyrannized by corruption. Therefore it says, "in this dwelling we groan" (2 Cor. 5:2). But when freedom appears they will rush to

Christ with an irresistible motion in order that they may receive their proper place. Accordingly Paul, as he shows that this rush cannot be restrained, calls it a "carrying up" [rapture], for he says, "we shall be carried off in the clouds to meet the Lord in the air" (1 Thess. 4:14). The Saviour says that He will take them to Himself: "then two men will be in the field; one is taken and the other left" (Mt. 24:20). This signifies that there is nothing human which will be able to delay, but that it is Christ Himself who will draw them, Christ Himself who will carry them off, He who cannot be subservient to time.

In the beginning He did not wait for men to seek Him, but sought them Himself as they were going astray. When He has shown them the way He then takes them up and carries them on His shoulders (Lk. 15:5) since they are not able to walk. He restores them when they have fallen and sets them upright when they have slackened and calls them back when they have gone astray and, in short, to the very end importunes them concerning their salvation. Likewise He Himself will raise them up as they run the last race towards Him, and will Himself make wings for them to fly. For this reason He also call us eagles which come together to the body when He says, "wherever the body is, there will the eagles be gathered together" (Mt. 24:28).

So they will move from one table to another, from that which is still veiled to that which is already manifested, from the bread to the Body. While they still live the human life Christ is bread for them, and He is their passover for they pass from here to the city which is in heaven. But when they "shall renew their strength, and mount up with wings like eagles," as says the admirable Isaiah (40:31), then they will take their position at the very Body which is unveiled. This also blessed John declares when he says, "we shall see Him as He is" (1 Jn. 3:2).

When the life in flesh has ceased Christ is no longer our bread, nor do we still await our passover. In His Body He bears many marks of His passion, for the hands bear the wounds and the feet bear the traces of the nails, and His side still bears the mark of the spear. This earthly banquet brings us to that Body. Apart from it we cannot receive the Body, any more than it is possible for one to look at the light whose eyes have been gouged out. If those who do not feast at this banquet have life in themselves, how could the Immortal One have become the Head of dead members [and have given them life]?

One only is the power of the table, one the Host in both worlds. The one world is the wedding feast with the Bridegroom Himself, the other is the preparation for that wedding feast. Accordingly, those who depart this life without the Eucharistic gifts will have nothing for that life. But those who have been able to receive the grace and preserve it have entered into the joy of their Lord (Mt. 25:21), and have gone in with the Bridegroom to the wedding feast (Mt. 25:10). Already they have enjoyed the other delight of the banquet though they do not obtain it fully yet; but when Christ has been manifested they will perceive more clearly what it is that they have brought with them.

This, then, is the account of how the kingdom of heaven is within us (Lk. 17:21).

THE FIFTH BOOK

*What the consecration
of the holy altar accomplishes*

[§ 1. The altar and the sacred Mysteries]

We have given an account of the sacred Mysteries, and of the preparation for the true life which they provide us. Now since the altar is the beginning from which every sacred rite proceeds, whether it be the partaking of the banquet or the reception of the anointing, whether it be ordination or the partaking of the most perfect gifts of the washing, then if we in addition to what has already been said, to the best of our ability examine the rite which sets up the altar, we shall not, I think, do anything superfluous or irrelevant. Rather, we shall then have given a more perfect account of that life, since we shall have given an account of the basis or root, or what ever else we may call it, of the Mysteries.

Let us therefore expound, in due order, all that happens at the hands of the celebrant in setting up the altar. Afterwards let us examine the hidden significance of each act and to what it points.

[§ 2. The ceremonies of consecration]

First, then, the hierarch* puts on white linen garments
and girds himself. He falls down and prostrates himself
before God on his hands and the rest of his body, yet not
on bare ground. After he has prayed that his effort may
obtain for him the desired end, he rises and proceeds with
the rite.

He lifts up the top of the table that was lying on the
ground and sets it on its base and affixes it. He himself
puts his hand to it, he does not merely order others to do it.
When he has placed it in position he washes it with warm
water, after praying that the water may have power to
cleanse it not merely from visible dirt but also from the
assault of demons.

He then anoints it by pouring on it some of the choicest
wine, and oil produced, I think, from the drippings of
roses. After these things he adds the sacred chrism and
anoints it therewith, tracing on the altar the sign of the
cross three times while he sings to God the celebrated prophetic song [i.e., Alleluia]. Then, after he has veiled it with
white linen he adorns it with rich hangings, and in addition
to these he unfolds other linens [i.e., the antimension] which,
like the table, have been anointed with the sacred chrism.
On these, which were the last to be placed on the table, the
sacred vessels must be set immediately.

When he has thus performed these ceremonies he loosens
and takes off his linen garments, and vested as a hierarch
he goes forth into a place adjoining the sacred buildings.
From there he takes the bones of holy martyrs made ready
for this very purpose, and places them upon either of the
vessels of the altar in which he would place the awesome
Gift [i.e., the Eucharist]. He covers them with that veil
which covers the oblation and with great reverence lifts them
up and carries them on his head. He goes forth with them

---

*Usually a bishop; otherwise one who has been specially delegated by
him, but who performs a somewhat curtailed rite.

to the house which is being consecrated, while the multitude honour his procession with torches, singing, and odours of incense.

Thus he comes forth, and when he reaches the temple and comes near to it he stands before the closed doors and commands those who stand within the doors to open them for the King of glory (Ps. 24:7, 9), as he utters the very words of David. When he has heard from those who are within the words which David represents the angels as saying to each other when the Saviour ascends into heaven, and when the doors are flung open, he enters into the temple with the veiled vessel upon his head.

When he has come within the altar [i.e., the sanctuary] and stands by the table itself he puts down the vessel and uncovers it. He removes the treasure contained therein and places it in a chest of appropriate size for the relics. After this he pours on them the most sacred chrism and deposits them under the table.

When these things have thus been prepared the house is a house of prayer, and the table is prepared for the sacrifice and belongs to it, and is properly an altar.

[§ 3. How the rites signify man's consecration to God]

Let us now explain the reason why these ceremonies are performed, and how, by the actions of the priest, the house and the table become what they are.

The hierarch approaching the sacred rite in his white linen garments is a vested type and image of the altar, which is man himself. If a man, as David says, "wash away all wickedness and become whiter than snow" (Ps. 51:9), and recollects himself and bends in on himself and bows down, that makes God truly dwell in the soul and makes the heart an altar. The ceremonies are the signs of these things. The first is indicated by his garment being white and shining, the second by him being altogether turned in on himself and bent down in body. Thus, as far as he is able, he exhibits

the altar in himself before he enters the sanctuary. After
this he puts the finishing touch upon the sacred place. This
is so because for the master workmen and, in fact, for all
craftsmen of any kind, it is reason which orders the task
before they put their hand to it. Reason supplies the plan
as a guide for the hands, they give expression to the plan
in the material.

It is the practice of painters to depict according to an
exemplar, in that they produce their art from preliminary
sketches, even when they use their memory for such things
and look to the soul for a model. Nor does this apply to
painters only, but one may see it in the case of sculptors,
architects, and indeed all craftsmen. Were it possible to see
the artificer's soul with the eye, one would see the (original)
house or statue or other work, apart from the material.

[§ 4. The meaning of the ceremonies of purification]

What makes the hierarch an exemplar of the altar is
not only that he is himself a craftsman of such things, but
that human nature, alone of things visible, is truly capable
of being a temple of God and an altar, since it preserves the
image and type of that which is fashioned by men's hands.

Accordingly it was necessary that in this pattern the
thing itself should appear before its image, and that the
reality should take precedence over the type. For He who
has said, "Would you build Me a house to dwell in?" (Acts
7:49), says, "I will make mine abode among them, and
walk among them" (Lev. 26:11, 12, 2 Cor. 6:16). This
means, I think, that it is fitting that he who would be of
help to others benefit himself first, and that he who is
enabled to cause so great a power to be infused into inanimate
objects must himself beforehand make such things to be of
avail to himself. So Paul thought it right that the bishop
who was to benefit a city and its environs should begin
from his own hearth, and that he who was to manage his
own household must, according to right reason, rule himself
first (1 Tim. 3:2-5).

But for this work he has need of God. No one would be able to achieve this or anything else without God's help, least of all the Mysteries in which everything is entirely God's work. Our common Master, however, did not provide for His servants merely by helpers, or by sending others to take care of them. He Himself came and achieved all that was needed for our salvation. For this reason the hierarch shows that he is His disciple and so fittingly with his own hand sets up the altar from which all the means of salvation flow to us.

This he does with the psalm "I will magnify Thee, O God my King" (Ps. 145) on his lips, as an act of thanksgiving to God and a memorial of His wondrous deeds. If the command of Paul bids us to give thanks in all things (Eph. 5:20), then how much more so must we when we deal with that which is the summary of good gifts? After this he adds another psalm, "The Lord is my shepherd, therefore shall I lack nothing" (Ps. 23). These words not only praise God's kindness to men, but touch the very benefits in question, for they mention Baptism and the sacred anointing and the chalice, and the table on which is the sacred bread. They call Baptism "the waters of comfort" and "green pastures," and state that he who is well shepherded by God will dwell with Him for ever. Since sin has brought trouble upon those who are presumptuous and has filled the earth with thorns for us (cf. Gen. 3:18), the water which casts out sin is the "water of comfort." The "green pastures" are the final resting place, because one may there receive God, the final good which we seek and in whom we rest. They may also be the waters of rest because they lay to rest the desire of our nature, of which Christ speaks when He says, "many prophets and kings have desired to see them" (Lk. 10:24).

Why then does not the hierarch, as he falls down before God and prays, at once touch the ground within the sacred precinct? Is it not because it has not yet received consecration and been made fit for the sacred rite? Since it has not yet become a house of prayer how can it fitly receive him who prays? Moses, on the other hand, when he was about to tread on holy ground had to take off his sandals so that he might bring nothing which might intervene in his meeting [with God] (cf. Ex. 3:5); while in Egypt the people of the Hebrews, who belonged to God, had to tread upon the ground shod with sandals (Ex. 12:11).

When the hierarch has prayed he proceeds to wipe the table clean with hallowed water. When the tyrant of all had enslaved man, the master of visible things, he assailed all sensible things as if they were a palace whose king had fallen. For this reason it is necessary to have a means of purification against the evil one to employ for all matter which is taken from nature for use in each of the Mysteries. As the priest first cleanses that water with which he who initiates must baptize from every abuse of demons by means of prayers and then adds to it the consecrating word, so likewise the hierarch first washes off the table with waters that fend off evil. Thus he points out the manner in which we must hasten to that which is good, that is, by first turning away from evil. For this cause he sings the psalm concerning human sin and repentance as he performs these rites, saying, "Thou shalt purge me with hyssop and I shall be clean; thou shalt wash me, and I shall be whiter than snow" (Ps. 51:7).

After that he gives thanks to God and reverences Him; and this he does in each of the acts of consecration. For it is needful that one do all to God's glory, and above all the Mysteries, inasmuch as they are more profitable than all other things and belong to God alone.

It is necessary, then, not only to be cleansed before receiving God's gifts of grace, but also, as far as we are able, to display the virtues which are in conformity with them. It is impossible otherwise to attain to the Giver of such gifts. (God grants the petition of him who prays, not of those who are asleep. He anoints him who enters the contest, and grants the gift of chastity to him who is chaste to his utmost ability. In short, in every case it is necessary to display our desire not merely by our prayers but in our actions.) Therefore, before he applies the most sacred chrism which is capable of bringing God's gift to the altar, the hierarch anoints the table with wine and oil, things which to us have a sweet smell. The latter merely provides us with delight, the former is also useful for life. This is to show that by bringing in all human things which fulfill our life, both those which are necessary for living and those which are pleasant, he offers the first fruits of both. Because Christ, when He came, both gave life and also gave it more abundantly (cf. Jn. 10:10), He not only raised up man and set him free, but made him a king by imparting the enjoyment which is undefiled. To these the hierarch adds the chrism which possesses all power for consecration* and straightway leads to the sacrifice.

[§ 5.   The meaning of the anointing of the altar]

Since, at the beginning, the Saviour accomplished the sacrifice with two actions when, as it says, "He took the bread and blessed" (Mk. 14:22), we too seek both that hand and that voice. That voice the priests utter and it is as effective as though it were He who commanded, "Do this for My memorial" (1 Cor. 11:24). The chrism has the power of that hand, for as the blessed Dionysius says, "the very chrism represents Jesus." But the apostles added their own hand, for they had the same gift. Those who succeeded them needed this initiation [i.e., the chrism], since they had only the power of the word. In the case of the first priests, their hands were an altar, but Christ built through those who came after them the houses which receive the initiates.

Now when he pours out the chrism on the table, unlike before, the hierarch accompanies it with no words. He merely sings that song to God which consists of a few syllables in the Hebrew tongue [i.e., Alleluia], yet is of the most sacred inspiration of the choir of the holy prophets. One might praise God's acts by describing them in a long discourse, or one might limit the songs to a few words and exalt Him who is the object of praise. It is fitting, I think, first that deeds already past or yet to come be so praised, so that the words might take the place of the actual deeds

---

*Possibly a reference here to the sacrament of Chrismation.

for those who contemplate them. The second method is fitting in the case of things that are present and happening now, for when the things themselves appear there is no need of words to proclaim them save to show how pleasant and wonderful they are. The prophets prophesied only until John appeared (Mt. 11:13). From thenceforward, what need was there of messengers when He appeared who had been announced beforehand? There was nothing left but to proclaim Him and to glorify Him. So thought the angels to whom He first appeared when He came to earth as their choirs sang, "Glory be to God in the highest" (Lk. 2:14).

According to this principle the hierarch, after he by his very acts has acknowledged Him who is called the Benefactor, neither prays anything that is contained in the preceding prayers nor recounts the works of His kindness as they stand before his eyes, but only glorifies them in the mystic song.

[§ 6. The appropriateness of the sacred relics]

Because the chrism is the power of the altar it was needful that the matter subject to it should be appropriate. Thus it would be more efficacious, just as also fire and light, I think, act through fitting bodies. For since the very name of the Saviour, which when invoked could do all things, did not manifest its power in the same way in the mouths of all men, therefore the consecrator, as he seeks whatever body might be fitting to subject to the chrism, has found nothing more suitable than the bones of martyrs. When he has anointed them and added them to the table he has perfected the altar.

There is nothing more akin to the Mysteries of Christ than the martyrs, since they have body, spirit, manner of death, and all other things in common with Christ. He was with them while they lived, and after they died He did not leave their dead bodies. He is so united to their souls that He is somehow present and mingled even with this mute dust. So, if it is possible to find the Saviour and to contain Him in any visible thing, it would be in these bones.

When, therefore, the hierarch comes to the temple he opens the doors for them with the same words which he would use if he were bringing in Christ Himself, and performs the other acts in the same way as he would honour the Holy Gifts. In addition, these bones are a true temple of God and an altar, while that which is made with hands is the imitation of the real. Wherefore it was reasonable to add the one to the other and to make use of it for the perfection of the other, just as in the case of the laws of the Old [Covenant] we add the New.

[§ 7.   The remaining sacred rites and their significance]

When the consecrator has completed all the ceremonies and prepared the house for the sacrifice and the prayers, and has lighted the lamp at the altar, he goes out. But first, I think, he shows by this the time of the sacrifice which was instituted at the beginning, for it was at eventide and at the time of the lighting of the lamps. Then, too, the lamp reminds us of that lamp which was in her house who had lost the coin, and how she found the coin after she lit the lamp and sought for that which was hidden by much earth and by darkness as though it lay under the earth in Hades. The sweeping of the house signifies, I think, that He who entered Hades and filled it with light uncovers all things and brings them into the light.

[And the hierarch anoints the whole house with chrism as he goes around it, in order that he may make it into a house of prayer and that the Name may be active and assist us for prayers. For the attendance of men upon God and that which directs our prayer as incense (Ps. 141:2) is the "ointment poured forth" (Cant. 1:3), the Saviour who has become our Advocate and Mediator towards God (cf. 1 Jn. 2:1). Since He is the only-begotten One He has poured Himself on His servants, thereby reconciling them to their Father who looks graciously upon us and draws near to those who draw near to Him, as though He finds in us the beloved Son Himself.

Whence it follows that God, who is invoked there, should come to the house in which we call upon Him and where the ointment of prayer is poured forth, and that, in accordance with Solomon's prayer, "His eyes should be open night and day toward this house" (1 Kgs. 8:29).

In yet another way the church is called a temple of God. In order that it might refer to the true Temple and have something in common with Him, it was necessary that as Christ was anointed with Godhead, so it should become an anointed thing by being anointed with the chrism. By the Temple of God I mean His most sacred Body, as He so called it by saying, "Destroy this temple" (Jn. 2:19, 21).]*

---

*An addition in the Vienna MS. in a different hand.

THE SIXTH BOOK

*How, when we have received grace
from the Holy Mysteries, we are to preserve it*

[§ 1. The necessity of preserving the grace
which we have received]

These Mysteries, then, are the things which belong to
the life in Christ and refer to Him, and pertain to Him
alone.

From the very beginning it depends on the Saviour's hand
alone that this life should come into being. Once it has been
established, its preservation, our continuance in life, depend
on our own efforts. So, in order that we may not destroy
the grace that we have received but preserve it to the end
and depart this life in possession of the treasure, there is
need of something human, of endeavour on our part. It
remains, then, that in the present discussion we examine
the means by which it is possible to achieve this preservation,
for this too suitably forms a part of our discourse on the
life in Christ.

In ordinary affairs it is neither reasonable nor usual
for us merely to be content with having received life, or to
fall asleep as though we possessed everything. Rather, we
must seek the means of preserving it. So likewise it is fitting

that we add a sequel to what we have said before concerning the origin and manner of our entrance into life and what we have experienced, and explain what we must do in order not to abandon our happy condition. It is this which is virtuous living according to right reason. But since it has been discussed at length by the ancients as well as by more recent writers, and they have omitted nothing which ought to have been said, we run the risk of performing a redundant task by completing this discussion. Yet the motives which impelled us at the beginning compel us to speak of these matters too, and it would be impossible for our discourse to be complete without them. We must then speak of them as we are able.

As is fitting, we omit the things which are proper to each different state of human life and examine the duties to God which we all have in common. No one would claim that the same virtues are needed by those who govern the state and those who live as private citizens, or by those who have made no further vow to God after the baptismal washing and those who live the monastic life and have taken vows of virginity and poverty and thus own neither property nor their own selves. But the debt which, like the very appellation itself, is common to all who are called by the name of Christ, must also be paid by all. Neglect of this debt on the part of anyone can be excused on no pretext whatever, whether of age, occupation, prosperity or adversity, remoteness, solitude, cities, or tumults—nor even by any of the numerous excuses in which those accused of crime take refuge. Nothing prevents anyone; all have the ability not to oppose the will of Christ, but instead to keep in every way the laws which derive from that will and to govern their lives in accordance with that which pleases Him. We may not claim that these things are beyond human ability, for then there would be no punishment for those who transgress.

Among Christians no one is unaware that he is under obligation to undertake the whole task. All alike, when they joined Him in the beginning, vowed to follow Him through all things, and it was after they had thus bound themselves

by those covenants that they underwent the sacred rites
[of Baptism].

Since the Saviour's commands are thus binding on all
the faithful and are capable of fulfilment by those who are
willing, they are most necessary. Apart from them it is impossible to be united with Christ, otherwise we should be at
variance with Him in that which is greatest and noblest,
will and purpose. If we share in His blood we must share
in His will. We cannot be joined to Him in some ways, and
yet be separated from Him in others, neither can we love
Him in one way and be hostile to Him in another, nor be
His children on the one hand and worthy of blame on the
other. Nor yet can we be His members, but be at the same
time dead ones for whom it avails nothing to be grafted
into Him and be born anew. This would be like the branch
which is severed from the true vine, whose end is to be cast
out and to wither and to be thrown on the fire (cf. Jn. 15:6).

[§ 2.   How we must cleave to Christ,
the Source of our life]

It follows, therefore, that he who has chosen to live in
Christ should cling to that Heart and that Head, for we
obtain life from no other source. But this is impossible for
those who do not will what He wills. It is necessary to
train one's purpose, as far as it is humanly possible, to conform
to Christ's will and to prepare oneself to desire what He
desires and to enjoy it, for it is impossible for contrary
desires to continue in one and the same heart. As He says,
"the evil man out of the evil treasure of his heart knows
how to produce nothing else but evil" (cf. Lk. 6:45), and
the good man that which is good.

The faithful in Palestine, since they desired the same
things, "were," as it says, "of one heart and soul" (Acts
4:32). In the same way, if one does not share in Christ's purpose but goes against that which He commands, he does not
order his life according to Christ's heart but is clearly
dependent on a different heart. In contrast, God found David

to be according to His heart, for he said, "I have not forgotten Thy commandments" (Ps. 119:16, 61, etc.). Since it
is impossible, then, to live [in Christ] unless we depend on
His heart, and one cannot depend on Him without willing
what He wills, let us examine how we may love the same
things as Christ and rejoice at the same things as He, in
order that we may be able to live.

[§ 3. How the love of Christ leads to
detachment from the things of earth]

The beginning, then, of every action is desire, and the
beginning of desire is reflection. Therefore we must above
all try to divert the eye of the soul from vain things by
having the heart always filled with good thoughts, so that
it at no time may give place to evil thoughts by being empty.

Since there are many things which are fit to supply matter
for contemplation, work for the soul, and delight and employment for the mind, it would appear that the consideration
of the Mysteries and the riches we derive from them would
be most pleasant and profitable both for speech and reflection. We may also reflect on what we were before we were
initiated and what we have become by being initiated, on
our former servitude and our present freedom and royal state,
on the benefits which have already been bestowed on us and
those which yet await us. Above all things we may think
on Him who is the Giver of all these gifts, how great is His
beauty, what is His kindness, how He has loved mankind
and how great is His love.

When these things which are so beautiful and attractive
take possession of the mind and take hold of the soul, it is
not easy to contemplate anything else and to transfer desire
towards a different object. His benefits overcome us by their
number and greatness, and the affection which moves Him to
bestow them is so great that the thoughts of men cannot
conceive it.

Just as human affection, when it abounds, overpowers
those who love and causes them to be beside themselves,

so God's love for men emptied God (Phil. 2:7). He does not stay in His own place and call the slave, He seeks him in person by coming down to him. He who is rich reaches the pauper's hovel, and He displays His love by approaching in person. He seeks love in return and does not withdraw when He is treated with disdain. He is not angry over ill treatment, but even when He has been repulsed He sits by the door (cf. Rev. 3:20) and does everything to show us that He loves, even enduring suffering and death to prove it.

Two things reveal him who loves and cause him to prevail—the one, that he in every possible way does good to the object of his love; the other, that he is willing, if need be, to endure terrible things for him and suffer pain. Of the two the latter would seem to be a far greater proof of friendship than the former. Yet it was not possible for God since He is incapable of suffering harm. Since He loves man it was possible for Him to confer benefits on him, yet it was not possible at all for the divine nature to suffer blows. While His affection was exceeding great, yet the sign by which He might make it plain was not available.

It was necessary, then, that the greatness of His love should not remain hidden, but that He should give the proof of the greatest love and by loving display the utmost measure of love. So He devised this self-emptying and carried it out, and made the instrument [i.e., Christ's human nature] by which He might be able to endure terrible things and to suffer pain. When He had thus proved by the things which He endured that He indeed loves exceedingly, He turned man, who had fled from the Good One because he had believed himself to be the object of hate, towards Himself.

But this is the most astounding thing of all. Not only did He endure the most terrible pains and die from His wounds, but also, after He came to life and raised up His body from corruption, He still retained those wounds. He bears the scars upon His body and with them appears to the eyes of the angels; He regards them as an ornament and rejoices to show how He suffered terrible things. While He discards the other features that belong to the body and possesses a spiritual body without weight or dimensions or

any other physical condition, He has by no means discarded
the scars, nor has He wholly rid Himself of the wounds. He
saw fit to cherish them because of His affection for man,
because by means of them He found him who was lost, and
by being wounded He laid hold on him whom He loved.
How else would it have been fitting for an immortal body
to retain the traces of wounds which art and nature have
sometimes eliminated even in mortal and corruptible bodies?
As it appears, He had the desire to suffer pain for us many
times over. Yet that was not possible, seeing that His body
had once for all escaped from corruption, and that He spared
the men who would have inflicted wounds on Him. So He
determined to preserve in His body the signs of His death
and always to have with Him the marks of the wounds
which were once inflicted on Him when He was crucified.
Thus it might be evident in the distant future that He had
been crucified and pierced in His side for the sake of His
servants, and together with His ineffable splendour He
might regard these too as an ornament for a King.

What could be equal to that affection? What has a man
ever loved so greatly? What mother ever loved so tenderly
(Is. 49:15), what father so loved his children? Who has
ever been seized by such a mania of love for anything beautiful whatever, so that because of it he not only willingly
allows himself to be wounded by the object of his love
without swerving from his affection towards the ungrateful
one, but even prizes the very wounds above everything?
Though these prove not only that He loves us but also that
He greatly honours us, yet it belongs to the greatest honour
that He is not ashamed even of the infirmities of our nature,
but is seated on His royal throne with the scars which He
has acquired from human weakness.

While He so highly esteemed our nature He yet did
not neglect us individually. He calls us all to His crown;
He has set us free from slavery and made us sons. He has
opened heaven to all, and has shown us the way and supplied
us with wings that we may fly thither. Not content with
this, He Himself leads the way and sustains us and encourages
us when we slacken.

Yet I have not mentioned the greatest thing of all. The Master is present with His servants not only to that extent, but He imparts of His own. He not only gives them a hand, but He has given us His whole Self. Wherefore we are the temple of the living God; our members are Christ's members whose Head the Cherubim adore. These very feet, these hands, depend on His Heart.

[§ 4. How Christ in His love is united to us]

What then can you meditate upon with greater profit and pleasure than these things? For when we examine them, and these thoughts prevail in the soul, no evil thoughts will gain entry into us. Then it will come about that, as we learn of His benefits, we will increase in longing for our Benefactor. When we thus greatly love Him we become keepers of His commandments and participants in His purpose, for as He says, "he who loves Me will keep My commandments" (Jn. 14:15, 21).

Besides, when we recognize how great is our own worth, we shall not readily betray it. We will not endure being slaves to a runaway slave when we have found out that a kingdom is ours. We shall not open our mouth in evil speech when we recollect the sacred banquet and that Blood which has reddened our tongue. How can we use our eyes to look on that which is not seemly when we have enjoyed such awesome Mysteries? We shall not move our feet nor stretch forth our hands to any wicked thing if the recollection of these things is active in our souls. Since they are members of Christ they are sacred, as it were a vial containing His Blood. Nay rather, they are wholly clothed with the Saviour Himself, not like a garment which we wear or the skin with which we are born, but much more, in that this clothing is far more closely united to those who wear it than their very bones. One could amputate our members without our consent, but as for Christ, no one, man or demon, can separate Him from us. As Paul says, "neither things present, nor things to come, nor height, nor depth, nor any other creature" (Rom. 8:38, 39), however great its power, can separate us from Him.

By means of tyrants' hands the evil one was able to tear off the skin of the martyrs of Christ, to mutilate their limbs and crush their bones and disembowel them. Yet so little did he by his designs avail to despoil the blessed ones of that garment and to denude them of Christ, that without realizing it he clothed them there with more than ever before by the very acts by which he thought to strip them.

[§ 5. How we should esteem ourselves as members of Christ]

What then could be more sacred than this body to which Christ adheres more closely than by any physical union? Accordingly we shall hold its high estate in veneration and preserve it when, conscious of so wondrous a splendour, we at all times hold it before the eyes of the soul. If we keep inviolate holy places and vessels and whatever else is sacred in all circumstances because we recognize their sacredness, we shall hardly betray things that are even greater. There is nothing so sacred as a human being to whom God has imparted of His nature. Consider this—to whom shall "every knee bow of things in heaven and things below the earth" (Phil. 2:10)? Who is it who "will come upon the clouds with power and great glory" (Mt. 24:30), shining with incomparable splendour? It will be a man, though certainly one like God. Each of us will then truly be able to shine more brightly than the sun, to rise on the clouds to see that body of God, to be uplifted to Him and fly towards Him, to approach Him and to be favourably regarded by Him. For when the Master appears the chorus of the good servants will surround Him, and when He shines brightly they too will shine.

What a sight—to see a countless multitude of luminaries above the clouds, an incomparable company of men exalted as a people of gods surrounding God! The fair ones surrounding the Fair One, the servants surrounding the Master!

He does not begrudge His servants if any of them share in His splendour, nor does He regard it as diminishing aught from His own glory were He to receive many as partakers of His kingdom. Those among men who hold others in subjection, even if they give their subjects everything, would not bear even to dream of them sharing their rule. But Christ does not regard His servants as though they were slaves, nor does He bestow on them honours fit for slaves; He regards them as friends. Towards them He observes rules of friendship which He has established from the beginning; He shares His own with them, not merely one or another part of His riches, but He gives the very kingdom, the very crown. What else is it that blessed Paul has in view when he says that they are "heirs of God and fellow heirs with Christ" (Rom. 8:17), and that all those who have shared hardships with Christ reign with Him (2 Tim. 2:12)?

What is so full of delight that it could vie with that vision of a chorus of blessed ones, a multitude of those who rejoice? Christ descends from heaven like lightning to earth, while the earth hands back other suns to the Sun of righteousness, and all is filled with light. From the earth come those who have shown zeal for Christ by their effort and endurance, their labours and their eagerness for such things. From the earth come those who have imitated His death and have surrendered themselves to swords and fire, still displaying the scars thereof on their radiant bodies and triumphing in the marks of their wounds as though they were the inscriptions on trophies of victory. They are a circle of champions who are illustrious by reason of their wounds, at the side of the King who by being slain has won the victory and, as Paul says, is "crowned with glory and honour because of the suffering of death" (Heb. 2:9).

[§ 6. **How love of Christ leads to true repentance**]

Having made this effort and used these opportunities for considering the matter we may arrive at a knowledge of the dignity of our nature, and also a clear perception of the loving-kindness of God. Indeed, this will prevent us from even looking at anything evil, and should we happen to fall it will readily raise us up again.

Of the many things which impede our salvation the greatest of all is that when we commit any transgression we do not at once turn back to God and ask forgiveness. Because we feel shame and fear we think that the way back to God is difficult, and that He is angry and ill-tempered towards us, and that there is need of great preparation if we wish to approach Him. But the loving-kindness of God utterly banishes this thought from the soul. What can prevent anyone who clearly knows how kind He is and that, as it is said, "while you are yet speaking He will say 'Here I am' " (Is. 58:9 LXX), from approaching Him at once for pardon of the sins which he has committed? This is a scheme and device against us on the part of our common enemy, that he moves him whom he leads into sin with rashness and daring, but inspires men with shame and ground-less fear once they have ventured on the most terrible deeds. Thus in the former case he prepares their fall, in the latter he does not permit them to rise anew, but rather both leads them away from God and prevents them from returning to Him. So he leads to the same ruin by opposite paths.

It is necessary, then, to beware of these things with all eagerness and to avoid the presumption before the sin no less than the shame and fear that follow it. They profit nothing, for this fear is not a spur to action but a stupor for our souls. We are not ashamed of our wounds in order that we may discover the means of healing, but rather in order that we may escape the eyes of the Saviour like Adam who hid himself (Gen. 3:8). On account of his wound he fled from the hand of the Physician whom he should have sought so that sin would not triumph over him, but by alleging his wife as an excuse he sought to cover up, as far as he could, the weakness of his will. After him Cain sought to be hidden by the means which he thought would hide him— and that from Him in whose sight are all things (Gen. 4:9)!

Now it is possible to have fear and shame and to humble one's soul and mortify one's body, and that with profit, when those things can lead to God. "You will know them," He says, "by their fruits" (Mt. 7:20). Now since grievous distress, even more than shame and fear, follows upon sin, no harm will come from this to those who rightly understand the loving-kindness of God. Even if they feel guilty of the ultimate wickedness they do not give up hope, knowing that no sin is too great for pardon or can overcome God's kindness. They endure salutary grief and seek to increase it; other grief they reject since it outrages good hopes.

There are two kinds of grief for transgressions, one which restores those who are afflicted by it, and one which brings ruin on them. Of both there are clear witnesses, the blessed Peter in the former case, the wretched Judas in the latter. The grief of the one preserved his purpose and commended him, after he wept bitterly to Christ no less than before he had sinned, whereas Judas's grief led him to the noose. When the blood was being shed which cleansed the whole world and all were being set free, he went off in bonds in despair of his own cleansing!

Since we know them beforehand let us welcome the former grief but flee from the latter. So we must look at the characteristics of both, how the former benefits us and the latter does us harm.

Because by sinning we commit an offence both against ourselves and against God it will by no means harm us to grieve over our presumption against the Master; indeed, it would be most opportune. In the case of the other, when we have formed high opinions of ourselves we see them refuted by the acts whereby we have offended against our duty; we are pained and mourn, and sore remorse oppresses the heart as though life were not worth living for those who have fallen into such great evils. From this grief it is necessary to desist. It is clearly the mother of death, as is also excessive self-esteem.

The former kind of grief derives from affection towards our Master. It makes us clearly to know our Benefactor and the things for which we are indebted to Him. Of the things for which we are His debtors we have not repaid even one; on the contrary, we have requited Him with evil.

Therefore, just as pride is an evil, so the pain which comes to our souls from the latter grief is an evil. On the other hand the love of Christ is altogether worthy of praise. Nothing is more blessed to those who are well-disposed than to suffer pain by reason of the darts which come from that love and to pine away in soul.

[§ 7. How we must constantly meditate on these things]

Thus the grief that is full of graces derives from love of Christ, and love depends on the thoughts which concern Christ and His loving-kindness. Accordingly it is profitable to hold these things fast in our memory and turn them over in the mind and at no time to desist from this occupation, but rather to be of set purpose to meditate and to reflect upon them when we are alone, and to make them the delight of our speech and the matter of conversation when we are with others. Besides, as far as it is possible, we should display this preoccupation without ceasing, or at least frequently, throughout our lives, so that it may be deeply imprinted on our hearts and completely possess them. Even fire, when it touches anything, can have no effect unless the contact continues; neither will occasional reflection dispose the heart to any affection. There is need of abundant and continuous time for this.

The reflections which proceed from beautiful and pleasant objects of sense enkindle desire, since our senses are active in us from the beginning and are our companions and associates. From them our reflections arise and readily persuade us whatever they will, both because they are pleasant and because they have been with us for a long time. Later in life, however, when we have arrived at understanding and its philosophy, much diligence is needed in order that we may be disposed to goodness in a short time, and constant attention as well, since such thoughts are not immediately attractive and have entered in late after many other things have filled the mind. It is only with difficulty and intense effort that we can break long-standing habits and introduce what is real in place of that which is merely apparent, and what is good in place of that which is merely pleasant. We need not then be surprised if the best thoughts do not in every instance prevail over evil thoughts, or if, for those who live by reason, the better thoughts do not avail more than the worse.

With good reason, then, I believe that it is not enough to learn persuasive arguments for virtue in order to be able to become virtuous, but that one must also spend time reflecting on it and constantly think thereon. One acquires right reason not merely by learning it, but also by employing it in necessary actions, just as food, weapons, medicine, and clothing are useful not merely by being at hand for those who possess them, but by their use.

But if evil thoughts occupy the mind and cause it to be busied with them, while we rush away at the perception of good thoughts as soon as we have merely tasted of them, is it any wonder that the worse prevail, and that the evil thoughts, by being active, will seize control of the soul while the good thoughts, by being inactive, are altogether cast out? It is not strange when a builder does not build, a physician does not practice, or any kind of craftsman is not engaged in his craft that he does not profit from it. Nor is it surprising that when anyone has right reason but does not exercise it he does not benefit. Were a man to use arms against invaders he would handle them to advantage, he would employ his skill aright by working in accordance with it. So we make use of the best thoughts as our counsellors by applying our mind not merely to acquire knowledge of them by study, but so that it may be convinced by this knowledge and acquire love of the things that are truly good. This requires elaborate care. On the other hand, being occupied with and employed in base things brings destruction to the soul, while mere knowledge about them is not dangerous. So, as it is necessary that we flee from the meditation of evil, we must pursue the meditation of that which is good.

Therefore it is no great effort to will what is good, since

it requires no prior diligence. But since it demands effort to take hold of it and to retain it, there is need of diligence and method. How may we readily undertake these struggles, since it is not easy to choose to suffer hardship?

In every case that which prepares us for the contest is the longing for the prize for which we contend. This makes the hardships pleasant, even when they are extremely painful. As for love of the good, nothing else will kindle it than turning one's mind to it and perceiving its beauty. This is the fire which was kindled in the prophet's soul by contemplation of God as he says, "as I mused the fire kindled" (Ps. 39:3). Elsewhere he shows that the subject of the meditation is God's law, and that it is the happy man who is occupied therein, for he says, "Blessed is the man," and "on His law he will meditate day and night" (Ps. 1:1, 2).

[§ 8.   The law of the Spirit is the law of love]

If meditation on the written law can kindle this fire, what then must be the effect of considering the law of the Spirit? It alone has inspired men with the true love of God and has kindled a fire which nothing can quench, neither adversities, nor things present, nor things to come. It is for this reason, I think, that the Spirit appeared "in tongues of fire" (Acts 2:3) when He came into the world, because He brought with Him a love which like fire dares all things. It is love which first brought to earth the Giver of the law, and the very body of this Lawgiver is the fruit of loving-kindness. Besides, His whole law is filled with love. He manifests this love with all that He has; He brings it into the world, by it He persuades, He accepts it as a sufficient recompense on our part for all that He has given.

So He does not command us as though we were slaves who owe Him a debt, but from the very beginning He calls those who come to Him into fellowship with Him, as though we had undergone many toils for Him beforehand and had enjoyed much friendship and intimacy with Him. So He summons us, "I have contended for the kingdom and have woven my crown with many toils, but you will receive it without toil. In return I ask of you that you love nothing more than you love me."

O unspeakable kindness! Not only does He love so greatly, but also He so highly esteems being loved by us that He does everything for the sake of this! What was the reason that He created heaven and earth, the sun and the visible world, and the beauty of the unseen world, and caused them to exist by His mere command? Does He not teach us the whole philosophy which derives therefrom in order that He may turn us to Himself and persuade us to love Him? In short, as ardent lovers do, He displays His wisdom, His kindness, and His skill in order to inspire us to love Him. Further, so greatly does He esteem the principle of the matter, so highly does He value it, that when He had made every effort befitting His divine nature to achieve our love He was not content therewith, but looked to another nature that He might employ it for His purpose. In order that He might be able to exercise whatever persuasion which was not open to Him because He is God, He became man. Thus, both by the nature which was proper to Him and by that which He assumed from us, He sought to attach to Himself the object of His love.

Thus the law of the Spirit is with reason a law of friendship and consequently trains us in gratitude.

[§ 9. How we must apply our minds to this law]

There is no toil involved in applying ourselves to this law, neither is it necessary to suffer hardship or to spend money, nor is there dishonour or shame, nor shall we be worse off in any other respect. It makes it no less possible to exercise our skills and it places no obstacle in the way of any occupation. The general may remain in command, the farmer may till the soil, the artisan may exercise his craft, and no one will have to desist from his usual employment because of it. One need not betake oneself to a remote spot,* nor eat unaccustomed food, nor even dress differently, nor ruin one's health nor venture on any reckless act. It is possible for one who stays at home and loses none of his possessions constantly to be engaged in the law of the Spirit.

What, then, prevents one from becoming virtuous in this way, for which virtue it would have been reasonable to endure hardship if necessary? If it is necessary for human beings capable of reflection to reflect in some way, why should they not reflect on the best things? If reflecting on vain and worthless things and on things that are of no use was never regarded as having an adverse effect on fortune, trade, wealth, or livelihood, least of all ought we to blame good thoughts for such effects and accuse that which is good of any ill whatever.

Indeed, good thoughts do not conflict with anything that is useful. So far from them partaking of anything disagreeable one might rather speak of them in terms of joy. If we then rejoice in the best things, nothing could be better than the thoughts of which the subject is Christ and His loving-kindness—not even the virtues which He supremely embodies, nor that which is pleasant and agreeable to ourselves. Even with great effort one would not find anything which is more suitable for us than these thoughts. As we have shown before, Christ is more akin to us not only than our blood relatives, but even than our parents and our very own selves.

Thus it follows that nothing is more appropriate to the thinking mind than thoughts concerning Christ. So one may say that the means of His intimacy and kinship with us are the best and most pleasant of all subjects for our reflection, the proper occupation of baptized souls. By these I mean those who have not become exceedingly hardened after the baptismal washing, like those Hebrews whom the

---

*Cabasilas here of course refers to the monastic life which he himself chose after his retirement—particularly in its most austere form, that of the hermits at Mount Athos and elsewhere who followed the venerable tradition of the Desert Fathers, particularly highly esteemed in the East as guides to sanctity.

admirable Stephen denounced as "uncircumcised in heart and ears" (Acts 7:51).

That from these thoughts no harm can come to human life, but rather that those who meditate on them benefit by pleasure and joy, is clear from what has been said. What profit there is in them and how they are to our best advantage has already been shown, and further, that they are the most excellent and timely things of all. From the closer examination which follows this will appear yet more clearly.

[§ 10. The spiritual profit of meditation on Christ]

First, then, restraining one's soul by good thoughts leads to cessation from evil thoughts. Similarly, the soul receives from the Mysteries a ray of light free of any weakness. Without any effort on our part it provides us with an abundance of all blessings.

Further, the very thoughts themselves must produce their effects by the remedies which they contain, and cause the heart to be occupied with the best things of all. Just as wicked thoughts give rise to evil passions, so likewise it is reasonable that good thoughts should give rise to virtue. In short, whether our purpose is the one or the other, whatever we intend to say or do or undergo, whatever choice we are to make, we are persuaded by reflections and reasonings. It is in this way that the teachers of virtue inspire their pupils as occasion serves: they inspire them to the best reflections. On the other hand, evil demons introduce evil impressions and in this way are instigators of the most unnatural deeds, while the former lead men to be active in the things they ought to do.

So it pertains to every laudable meditation to make use of Christ's acts for virtue, to reflect on Christ and the things which He in loving-kindness has devised for my salvation. This contains the very life that we seek and in all respects makes us blessed. In order that we may know this clearly let us contemplate the conditions which have been fulfilled

by those whom Christ Himself called blessed, whether they
do not all depend on these reflections.

[§ 11.   On the Beatitudes of Christ]

Who then are these whom He calls happy, who alone
are truly blessed? Those who are poor in spirit, those who
mourn, those who are meek, those who hunger and thirst
for righteousness, those who are merciful, those who are
pure in heart, those who are peacemakers, those who endure
persecutions and every reproach for their righteousness and
zeal for Christ. Such are they who have laid hold on the
blessed life. If, therefore, we proceed from these reflections
and in our examination find that the chorus of saints has
been transformed according to that noble model, and that
their crowns have been pleated by these thoughts, it will be
quite evident to everyone that the study and meditation of
these reasonings is a sure passage leading to the blessed life,
a ladder by which we may ascend to it, or whatever other
figure of speech we may employ.

[a.   The first Beatitude—poverty of spirit]

For example, "poverty of spirit" is, as Paul says, "not to
think more highly than one ought to think, but to think
soberly" (Rom. 12:3). To whom would this pertain except
those who understand the poverty of Christ? Although He
was the Master, yet He shared with slaves their nature and
ways of life. Though He is God, yet He "became flesh"
(Jn. 1:14). He who was rich chose poverty, the King of
glory endured dishonour, and He who had set mankind free
was led about in chains. He was indicted for lawless deeds
though He had come to fulfil the law. He to whom "the
Father had given all judgment" (Jn. 5:22) endured judges
who gratified a maddened and murderous mob. What con-
ceit would not be brought low by these things?

Furthermore, whenever deeds which seem to excel in

virtue become the occasion for pride, he who has meditated on the deeds of Christ will know that not only has he achieved nothing great, but that he has availed to contribute nothing at all to his release from captivity, let alone preserve his freedom inviolate after his release. It is Christ who has redeemed us with His Blood and granted us freedom after purchasing it at so great a price. But who of those who have been freed has remained in the freedom which he has received? And who has kept the spiritual riches inviolate to the end? Is not only he who has committed minor offences against grace regarded as very virtuous? What reason will there be for us to think highly of ourselves when we are conscious of sin, and when our virtue by itself leads to nothing that profits us? If there is any true goodness in us, God has implanted it without any effort on our part. We are so worthless that we are unable to guard even the riches imparted from without as if they were an inanimate treasure. After the new creation and the burial in water and the table that is full of fire even the wisest men are so weak in virtue that they stand in constant need of the holy table and the cleansing Blood and the helping hand from above, if they are not to be carried away into the utmost wickedness.

Of this there are sure witnesses, men who were ready for every effort of goodness and virtue, and yet afterwards ventured on desperate evil. They had betaken themselves to the mountains and fled from every disturbance and from ordinary living as though they were evil diseases in order to pay attention to God alone. As far as man is able they had attained the highest virtues and were able to achieve the greatest things for God. Yet when they slackened but a little from their hope in Him and from trusting Him in all things they forthwith ventured on the most shameful deeds and shrank from no wickedness whatever.

How then shall we think proudly? Because of our good deeds? But we have done nothing that is great! Because of our merits? But they are not our own! Because we have preserved what we have received? We have betrayed it! Is it that we bear Christ's seal? This pride is the very proof

that we do not bear it, for those who are proud have nothing
in common with Him who "is meek and lowly in heart"
(Mt. 11:29). By these thoughts pride collapses on itself and
is vanquished from all sides. Either we think what we ought
to think, or else we think proudly. When we perceive that
by proud thoughts we are far removed from Christ and there
is no health in us we shall realize that we are worthless and
not think proudly.

[b. The second Beatitude—godly sorrow]

It is indeed fitting that those who meditate on Christ's
deeds mourn and weep. Were one to consider what novel
things were accomplished for our salvation, what would
happen to our indifference and the sleep which detains us?
Whether we are grieved at the loss of things most precious,
or constrained to weep by the memory of good things which
we have lost, this is the way that we learn how great are
the riches we possess, how it is possible to retain them,
and how we may waste them. Or if our conscience prick
the soul and cause it to waste away because we are ungrateful
towards so great a Benefactor, it is in this way that it would
become most clear to us how great is the gentleness and
loving-kindness with which He has dealt with us, and how
great is the indifference we have shown to Him.

First, He came down from heaven to seek us. He spoke
to us with a voice like ours and appeared to us with a face
like ours. This He did in order that, whether it is the one
like ourselves that we love or the One who is the best, He
Himself might be both. Thus by uniting in Himself the two
which everywhere inspire love He sought the means of
inspiring the greatest love.

Further, He added this also in order to increase this
friendship: Since everyone loves himself and also loves his
kin, yet, being much closer to himself than to his fellow-
man, he cares more for himself than for his neighbour—so,
with the aim of being in the best position for receiving our
love, which is the most desirable thing of all, and thus to

be loved, not in the way that we rejoice over our fellow men, but in the way that we are objects of our own love, He was not content to become like us by sharing in our nature, but imparted to us His very Body and Blood and Spirit so that He might thus be loved by all men. Thus He Himself becomes in actuality that which the proverb says concerning our friends in exaggeration—the "other self" of every one who cleaves to Him.

Thus it was that He sought us and left nothing undone which pertained to this friendship. He showed Himself as our Benefactor and Brother. He took the place of our very selves, not merely in will or by the command by which He created the heavens, but by the sweat of His brow and by toils which were entirely alien to Him, by agony, by dishonour and stripes, and finally by death. Yet towards Him who thus is good to us in every way we have not only forgotten gratitude and failed to seek how we may require Him, but we behave so badly that we are devoted to the things which are hateful to Him and cleave to the things from which He turns away. As for the things to which He urges us we flee from them, and thus display unnatural wickedness. Is this not worthy of laments and tears? We highly esteem other things, but neglect the Saviour and that which is His as though it befitted others to seek Him, or as though His unutterable providence had nothing to do with us.

As for the things which are useful to us, we regard it our duty to use them as we ought. In all the things which have to do with living, all words, acts, and skills, whether we must farm or command an army, whether they pertain to public affairs or to one's personal life, in every case we seek what is fitting and embrace the right opportunity. In short, everywhere we highly value that which is customary, fitting, and just. It is only in the case of that which is truly our own—how we ought to guard it as we should, by what means we must do justice to ourselves—that we consider these things least of all, as though we regarded ourselves inferior to everything else!

If for no other reason, we should turn our attention to that novelty which has shaken and displaced all things.

Because of it the very foundations of the earth have seen the things which are above heaven, and earth has ascended above heaven itself. The tyrant of the whole world became a captive, and the former prisoners tread the tyrant's head under foot. God was seen to be wearing a body, one that submitted to stripes and shed its blood upon the cross. Further, the dead body of a man shook the earth and restored life to the dead without any effort on their part but that of recognizing the Master and rising from the earth and looking towards heaven at that man. Who, then, are more wretched than those who, after these things have happened, still are asleep like statues, unaffected by claps of thunder?

But how should the righteous fail to regard the whole time of this life as an opportunity for sorrow? What then do we bewail? Is it disease? In our case, is not the best part diseased? Is it poverty? Indeed, in this respect we are far worse off than the poor, since spiritual wealth is more necessary and excellent by far. Material poverty must presently cease, but death cannot destroy the terror of spiritual poverty but rather must greatly increase our disgrace in the life to come. Madness is miserable. What then? Does not a wicked demon harrass the mind into which it has poured so great a measure of folly? If rushing upon the sword, casting themselves down from steep heights, ignoring their friends and fawning upon their worst enemies, are acts of madmen, then are we not also mad for fleeing from Him who loves us, and do we not seek our enemy by our actions? Are we not hastening to hell by doing all the things which drive us to it?

Thus, since we have the most horrible things on our consciences, it is fitting for us to weep and mourn. Would that we could become conscious of these things and consider our true condition! We should not be so wretched then, by being ignorant of the evils in which we find ourselves, if we knew the sound health and the riches and the sanity of mind which could be ours without any effort, since Christ provides them and we contribute nothing but our willingness. But it would gnaw at one's heart the more that it was possible for one to enjoy happiness but had chosen misery, the more that one who was able to dwell in the light should endure to sit in darkness.

It is not merely the sluggish whom these things may move to tears, but especially the most virtuous, since they are most keenly aware of the loss. For even those who blame themselves for still worse offences and regard themselves as deserving the worst penalties are moved thereby, when they think how God, whom all things serve, was stripped naked and slain upon the cross, and that He demands from us an appropriate recompense. Since He Himself took man's nature though He was God, we should become gods instead of men and exchange earth for heaven, slavery for a kingdom, our accustomed dishonour for the true glory. For the sake of these things it was that the Creator of heaven clothed Himself with earth, and that He who by nature was Lord "was found in the fashion of a slave" (Phil. 2:6, 7), and the King of glory "endured the cross, despising the shame" (Heb. 12:2).

[c. The third Beatitude—gentleness]

Of the many examples whereby the Saviour brought the true philosophy into the world, the most and the greatest of all were the examples which He gave of gentleness, restraint of anger, and patient endurance of those who grieved Him, by means of His actions and the sufferings which He endured. For example, on behalf of those who had grieved Him He was content to partake of blood and flesh; He came to seek and set free the very men whom He could have indicted for the most heinous offences. At their hands He afterwards received reproaches for the good deeds by which He restored our nature, yet He ceased not to do them good. Because He cast out the demons from men He heard Himself called Beelzebul and the ruler of demons (Mt. 9:34) and the worst names of all; yet nevertheless He drove them out. So far from casting out one who was disaffected with Him from the company of the disciples, He conversed with him as is proper to friends. Even though He was taken prisoner He had dealings with the murderer and the betrayer of His secrets and of His blood, and finally gave Himself to be embraced and kissed.

Even then He ventured on that which was most novel of all—He died for those to whom He had done good. The recipients of benefits drew the sword, the friend led the murderers in the act of murder, the kiss was the signal for the betrayal. He who underwent these things behaved Himself so gently and lovingly, that when one of the disciples had wounded one of those bestial men He did not ignore his wound but at once healed it by touching the member. When He had thus given a sign both of His extraordinary power and of utmost gentleness He did not destroy those who neither feared the one nor respected the other. He did not rain fire upon the wretches nor cast thunderbolts on them, worthy as they were of these and even worse punishments.

He whom the hosts of angels could not behold without fear followed those who dragged Him off. The hands to which the bonds of disease had yielded and by which the tyranny of demons was broken, He presented to be bound. Though He was able to do so, He did not destroy that most wicked and desperate slave who struck His cheek, but thought him worthy of being addressed most gently and kindly and, as far as He was able, He corrected his ill will.

He then in silence endured the sentence of those brutal judges who had condemned Him to death. When He had accepted the penalty and was already nailed to the tree He did not desist from His affection for His murderers, but went as far as to implore His Father to exact no penalty from them for their atrocity against the only-begotten One. He not merely interceded for them but defended them. The voice of the defence came from One who was burning with exceeding mercy, for He said, "Forgive them, Father, for they know not what they do" (Lk. 23:34). Just as a father who loves his children is sorry for them when they are foolish because of their tender age, so He made their Chastener be gentle towards them, and then died with these words on His lips.

After He returned to life He received those of His friends who had continued in their purpose to share in the festal joy. He bore them no grudge for having deserted Him and fled at the height of perils. So He called His disciples together and made known to them where they should assemble and meet with Him. When He met them and appeared to them He did not reproach them for their flight. It does not appear anywhere that He remembered any such thing against them— how they had all affirmed that they would share death and the uttermost extremity with Him, yet could not endure the thought of the terrors even before they happened. He bestowed upon them peace and the Holy Spirit and similar blessings, and then entrusted to them the care of the whole world and set them up as rulers over all the earth.

These things He did to all their company. What things did He for the very leader, who had often betrayed the affection that He bore him and had denied His love? Not only did He forbear to expose his denial—He did not remind him of his pledge which he had forsworn by failing to join his Teacher in death, that pledge which he broke so short a time later—but to him, apart from the others, he sent the messengers of His resurrection and so did him honour. When He encountered him He conversed with him as befits a friend and asked him whether his love for Him was greater than that of His other friends. When Peter said that he loved Him He again asked him, and when He heard him say, "I love you" (Jn. 21:16), He again asked whether He was loved by him. He might, I think, have asked many times over, had not Peter been grieved and refused to answer further, as though there were need of many words for Him who knows all things to find out that He was loved.

These were not the actions of one who did not know a friend or pretended not to know him. In the former case He would have been mistaken, in the latter He would have been deceitful, neither of which was possible. Rather He wished to show thereby that He bore no ill will for the past confessions which had been violated, for He did not look for a second one but rekindled in Peter the affection which was in danger of shortly being extinguished. To ask such

questions and elicit such replies is more effective for friendship than anything else, and the memory of proofs of friendship and speaking of such is capable not only of making it
greater than before, but even of evoking it where it has not
yet begun.

Thus it is manifest by His deeds that the Saviour has
cast out anger. Is there anyone then who surpasses Him in
gentleness as He teaches and gives laws? He goes so far
as to say that when we are angry with anyone He will not
accept even the prayer which we utter and the sacrifice which
we offer. Of the forgiveness of sins, which He came from
heaven to bestow on us as a gift common to all, He says
that He will never grant it to those who are angry at each
other even though we do everything to obtain it, even if
we pour forth floods of sweat and tears, even if we give
our very body over to the sword and to fire (cf. 1 Cor.
13:3)—so high is the value that He sets on gentleness.

So it follows that those who reflect on the things that
are His should have a heart which is gentle towards those
who grieve them. This too He shows by meaning in effect,
"If you know how gentle I am, your heart also will become
thus," when He says, "Learn from me; for I am gentle and
lowly in heart, and you will find rest for your souls" (Mt.
11:29).

Further, in the following way as well gentleness may
result from meditation on Christ. He who lives in these
thoughts must be inflamed with love of the holy table,
but from it one may not receive when one bears ill will. So
he will stand firm and keep his soul pure from hatred, since
this Blood which was first shed for reconciliation will not
endure those who are slaves to anger and wrath, and rightly
so. Even though He lifted up His voice to the Father concerning His murderers, as did Abel's blood when it was shed,
yet He bore no accusation to Him against the wrongdoers nor
asked for their punishment as did Abel for that of his brother.
This Blood truly redeemed, and His voice brought pardon
to those who slew Him.

[d. The fourth Beatitude—hunger and thirst for righteousness]

Furthermore, those who live with such thoughts are, more than all other men, workers of righteousness. In them it is apparent that the Ruler of the world has so greatly honoured righteousness, that He came among the slaves, among condemned criminals, among those who were being put to death, among the dead, in order that He might render to all what was just. No one else was able to render to the Father the glory and obedience which were due to Him from of old, and to render to the tyrant the chains, contempt, and shame by which Christ destroyed his unjust dominion, and drove out the usurper and brought him down by judgment and righteousness.

[e. The fifth Beatitude—compassion]

From what other source than these considerations would one derive mercy, the sharing of pain with those who suffer, the regarding of the misfortunes of others as one's own? By them we see ourselves as those who least of all deserve mercy, yet have received mercy beyond all expectation by being set free from that captivity, that slavery, those bonds, and the madness of him who enslaved us. The tyrant never limited the evils whereby he afflicted us, but we found him constantly harsher and worse, while we were helpless and forsaken on all sides and without any who could give us a helping hand. He was able to pursue his purpose against us and led us off as though we had been sold into bondage. Neither from ourselves nor from elsewhere, whether from those above us or from our equals, had we any solace or remedy for these terrors, but for all it was equally impossible to be of help to the human race. What remedy could I mention for those for whom it was plainly impossible to be mindful of the Physician or to implore His aid?

Since, therefore, we were in so miserable a state, it was no messenger or angel but the Lord Himself with whom we were at war. He whom we were offending by breaking His law had compassion on us with unwonted mercy beyond all reason and all that was fitting. Nor did He merely will for us deliverance from evils or regard our sorrow as His own. He appropriated our pains and transferred them from us to Himself, having Himself undertaken to appear and to act in a manner worthy of mercy in order that He might make us blessed. For, as Paul said, "in the days of His flesh" (Heb. 5:7) He seemed to many to be among those who should be pitied, and He was the object of pity as He died the unjust death, for as it says, "they bewailed and lamented Him" (Lk. 23:27) as He was being led to His death. Nor did this apply merely to those who lived then and witnessed the passion, but already Isaiah, seeing it from afar, endured not the sight without tears. Like one who sings a solitary lament for the dead He uttered a voice full of pity, saying, "we saw him, but he had no form or comeliness, his appearance was dishonourable, his appearance was failing beyond the sons of men" (53:2-3 LXX).

What could equal this compassion? He shared the suffering of the unfortunate not merely in thoughts and in will, but in very deed. He was not content merely with sharing in misfortunes, but took all on Himself and died our own death. If previous experience of any misfortune disposes us kindly towards those who are now suffering equal ills so that we make their calamities our own, what is it that we can not have suffered? Is it the loss of our true native land? Is it poverty and disease? Is it the most cruel bondage, the very limit of madness? From all these things we have been delivered "through the tender mercy of our God" (Lk. 1:79). Should we not therefore pity ourselves when someone suffers misfortune in any of these ways, and should we not show that pity to our fellow servants which the Ruler of all first had towards us (cf. Mt. 18:33)? The Saviour makes it clear that it is indeed necessary to be kind to our fellow men as we look on the pattern of the divine loving-kindness when He says, "be merciful, even as your Father is merciful" (Lk. 6:36).

[f. The sixth Beatitude—purity of heart]

To cleanse one's heart and to exercise one's soul for sanctification—what striving or effort or exertion would effect this more than these thoughts and meditations? Yet, if one examines this carefully, one would not call it the effect of meditation on Christ, but rather of the meditation itself.

To be occupied with the noblest of thoughts means to abandon evil thoughts; but this is to be pure in heart. Our life and our birth are twofold, both spiritual and fleshly. By its desires, the spirit fights against the body and the body resists the spirit. Since it is impossible for contraries to be at peace and to join together, it is quite evident that one or other of the desires will, by means of memory, gain control over the thoughts and cast the other out. The memory of the life and birth which are according to the flesh and concentration on such matters produce the most depraved desires and the uncleanness to which it leads. So likewise, when the soul by constant remembrance holds fast the birth of the baptismal washing, the divine Food which is appropriate to this birth, and the other things which belong to the new life, it is likely to lead desires from the earth to heaven itself.

[g. The seventh Beatitude—striving for peace]

Since Christ "is our peace, who has made both one, and has broken down the dividing wall, the hostility in the flesh" (Eph. 2:14), who planned all things for the sake of peace, what would come before that peace for those who highly esteem the care of the soul and are eager for that which is His? Above all else they will "strive for peace" (Heb. 12:14, cf. Rom. 14:19), as Paul commands, and will be leaders in this matter for others. They will cast away useless hostility and will stop those who are rashly at war, knowing that peace is so precious a thing that God Himself came to the earth for the purpose of purchasing it for men. Though He was rich and the Lord of all He found no price sufficient for it but that of shedding His own blood. Since He found those who were already born in possession of no just equivalent for the peace and reconciliation which He sought, He created a new creature for Himself, His blood. By giving this He at once became the reconciler and the Prince of peace. Those, then, who worship that blood, hope to achieve, beyond their own salvation, peace for men as agents of reconciliation.

Thus it is possible to discern in the character of the only Saviour the whole of righteousness, that is, virtue, and how great a benefit it is and what beauty it contains. He alone has exhibited a character totally pure from all that is contrary to virtue, for "He committed no sin" (1 Pet. 2:22). Nor, when the "ruler of the world" came, did he find anything for which he might persecute that divine soul, nor anything with which he might fault His beauty as he looked at Him from all sides with an envious eye. It is obvious that it is possible for those who meditate on the things of Christ to be kindled with love for Christ and for virtue by that alone. The result will thus be that one understands the beauty of virtue and of the Saviour, and those who understand will also love, since to understand always leads to love. It was instead the deceptive fruit of the forbidden tree which overpowered Eve, for it says, "she perceived that it was a delight to the eyes and good for food" (Gen. 3:6).

[h. The eighth Beatitude—suffering reproach for Christ]

When we have thus received love for Christ and for virtue it is fitting that we should endure persecutions for their sake and even, if need be, choose to flee the world and to be the object of the most horrible accusations, and that gladly, since the greatest and fairest rewards are laid up for us in heaven.

The love of those who contend for Him who awards the prizes is able to effect even this. It causes them to put their trust in Him for the prizes which do not yet appear and to have constant hope in the present for that which is to come. It makes those who at all times reflect and meditate on the things of Christ so temperate and mindful of human weakness that they mourn. It makes them gentle and just, benevolent and sober, peacemakers and reconcilers of men. Thus they will so cleave to Christ and to virtue that for their sake they will not only bear insults, but rejoice over them and gladly be persecuted. In short, from these reflections it is possible to enjoy the greatest benefits by which we may become blessed, and so preserve the will in goodness and the noble soul in the beauty which it has attained, and to guard the riches derived from the Mysteries, neither rending nor defiling the royal vesture.

Therefore, as it is proper to human nature to have a mind and to use reason, so it is necessary to regard the contemplation of the things of Christ as the proper function of reasoning. This is so, particularly because Jesus alone is the pattern to which men must look, whether they are to do anything for themselves or lead others in the performance of duty. In the beginning, in the middle, and at the end, for personal living and for public affairs alike, He has shown men true righteousness.

In addition, He Himself is the prize and the crown whom those who contend are to receive. We must therefore look to Him and carefully examine the prizes which belong to Him, and as far as possible learn to understand them, so that we may know how we must strive for them. Athletes regard the contests in terms of the prizes that are offered and so endure toils and exhibit perseverance to the extent that they have perceived them to be great. Besides all these things, who does not know how great is the price for which Christ acquired possession of us? He alone purchased us with His own blood, therefore there is no other whom we must serve and for whom we must employ ourselves, body and soul alike, as well as give all our love, our memory, and our mental activity. For this reason also Paul says, "you are not your own; you were bought with a price" (1 Cor. 6:19-20).

[§ 12. Christ the Exemplar of our perfection]

It was for the new man that human nature was created at the beginning, and for him mind and desire were prepared. Our reason we have received in order that we may know Christ, our desire in order that we might hasten to Him. We have memory in order that we may carry Him in us, since He Himself is the Archetype for those who are created. It was not the old Adam who was the model for the new, but the new Adam for the old, even though it is said that the new Adam was generated according to the likeness of the old (Rom. 8:3) because of the corruption which the old Adam initiated. The latter Adam inherited it in order that He might abolish the infirmity of our nature by means of the remedies which He brings and, as Paul says, so "that which is mortal might be swallowed up by life" (2 Cor. 5:4).

For those who have known him first, the old Adam is the archetype because of our fallen nature. But for Him who sees all things before they exist the first Adam is the imitation of the second. It was in accordance with His pattern and image that he was formed, but he did not continue thus. Rather, he started to go in His direction but failed to attain to Him. Accordingly, it was the former who received the law but the latter who fulfilled it. Of the old Adam obedience was demanded; the new Adam, as Paul says, displayed it "unto death, even death on a cross" (Phil. 2:8). The one by transgressing the law manifested himself as lacking the things which are required of man, for the law for which the transgressor was liable to punishment did not surpass nature. But the second Adam was perfect in all things and, as He says, "I have kept my Father's commandments" (Jn. 15:10). The former introduced an imperfect life which needed countless aid, the latter became the Father of immortal life for men. Our nature from the beginning tended to immortality; it achieved it much later in the body of the Saviour who, when He had risen to immortal life from the dead, became the leader of immortality for our race.

To sum it up: the Saviour first and alone showed to us

the true man, who is perfect on account of both character and life and in all other respects as well.

Since incorruptible life is truly the end of man, God formed him with a view to this goal. It became possible after his body became pure from corruption and his will free from all sin. The perfection of anything consists in this, that the craftsman makes it all that he thinks it should be, as when the beauty of a statue is achieved by the final touch of the sculptor's hand. But while the former Adam fell greatly short of perfection, the latter was perfect in all respects and imparted perfection to men and adapted the whole human race to Himself. How then would the latter not be the model of the former? We must, then, regard Christ as the Archetype and the former Adam as derived from Him. For it is most absurd to regard the most perfect of all things as striving towards the imperfect, and to posit the inferior as the model of the superior, as though the blind were to lead those who see!

It is not surprising that the imperfect is prior in time when we consider that many things were prepared in advance for the use of men and that man who is the measure of all these came from the earth last of all. But it is fitting to believe that the perfect is the first principle of the imperfect by reason of its perfection.

So then, for all these reasons man strives for Christ by nature, by his will, by his thoughts, not only because of His Godhead which is the goal of all things, but because of His human nature as well. He is the resting place of human desires; He is the food of our thoughts. To love anything besides Him or to meditate on it is a manifest aberration from duty and a turning aside from the first principles of our nature.

[§ 13. How meditation is based on constant prayer]

But that we may be able to have our attention always directed towards Him and have this zeal at all times, let us call on Him, the subject of our reflections, at every hour.

There is no need whatever of special formalities for prayers, nor need those who call upon him have any special places or a loud voice. There is no place in which He is not present; it is impossible for Him not to be near us. For those who seek Him He is actually closer than their very heart.

It follows, then, that we should firmly believe that our prayers will have results. We should not waver because of our sinful condition, but rather take courage because He on whom we call is "kind to the ungrateful and the wicked" (Lk. 6:35). So far is He from ignoring the entreaties of His servants who have offended Him, that before they call on Him or pay any heed to Him, He Himself has already called them, in that He Himself came to the earth—for He said, "I came to call sinners" (Mt. 9:13).

How then will He, who thus sought those who did not even desire Him, treat those who call on Him? If He loved even though He was the object of hatred, how will He disdain us when we love Him? This Paul makes clear when he says, "if while we were enemies we were reconciled to God by the death of His Son, much more, now that we are reconciled, shall we be saved by His life" (Rom. 5:10).

Let us also consider the form of our supplication. We do not ask for the things which friends properly ask for and receive, but rather for such things as above all belong to those who are subject to judgment, to slaves who have offended their Master. For we do not call upon the Master in order that He may reward us or bestow any favour upon us, but that He may have mercy. By whom, then, is it proper to ask for mercy, pardon, remission of sins and suchlike from Him who loves men, that they may not depart with empty hands? Those who are under judgment, since "those who are well have no need of a physician" (Mt. 9:12). Since it is the general practice that when men lift up their voices to God they should appeal for mercy, they raise their voices who have acted so as to need mercy, who have committed sins.

So we call on God with voice, mind, and thoughts in order that there may be applied the only saving remedy for all our sins, for as it says, "there is no other name by which we must be saved" (Acts 4:12).

[§ 14. The benefits of frequent Communion]

Now the true Bread who "strengthens the heart of man" (Ps. 104:15) and came down from heaven bringing us life (cf. Jn. 6:32-33) will suffice for all things. He will intensify our eagerness and take away the inborn sluggishness of the soul. Him we must seek in every way in order that we may feed on Him and ward off hunger by constantly attending this banquet. Nor should we unnecessarily abstain from the holy table and thus greatly weaken our souls on the pretext that we are not really worthy of the Mysteries. Rather, we must resort to the priests [for Confession] on account of our sins so that we may drink of the cleansing Blood.

But if we know these things we should by no means incur guilt from great offences so as to be excluded from the holy table. It is the ungodly who insolently approach the sacred Gifts after committing a sin unto death; those who are not afflicted with such diseases may not rightly flee from that Bread. For those who are still in their wills fighting its coals it is right to beware of the Fire and not receive Christ to dwell with them until they have been reconciled to Him. Those whose wills are rightly disposed but who are sickly in other respects have need of the strengthening medicine, and should betake themselves to Him who bestows spiritual health, and who "has borne our infirmities and carried our diseases" (Is. 53:4), rather than shun Him who will heal them on the pretext of their ailments.

Christ's Blood, then, closes the doors of our senses and allows nothing to pass through them which is able to harm us. Nay more, by sealing the doors it wards off the destroyer (cf. Ex. 12:13) and makes the heart into which it has been poured a temple of God. It is better than the walls of Solomon, which are a type of that Blood, in that it prevents the evil idol, "the abomination of desolation in the holy place" (Mt. 24:15), from being set up. It strengthens the mind "with a governing spirit" (Ps. 51:12 LXX), as David says, and subdues the mind of the flesh to it so that man may enjoy profound calm.

But since it has already been treated at length there is no need for me to prolong the discussion of this Mystery and of its effects for those who have been initiated. If we are thus with Christ by sacred rite, prayer, meditation, and reflection, we shall train the soul for every virtue. As Paul commands, we shall "guard what has been entrusted to us" (1 Tim. 6:20) and preserve the grace which has been imparted to us from the Mysteries. It is Christ Himself who initiates us in His Mysteries; He Himself is the content of the Mysteries. Likewise it is He who preserves His gifts in us. It is He alone who enables us to abide in that which we have received, for as He says, "apart from me you can do nothing" (Jn. 15:5).

THE SEVENTH BOOK

*What manner of man one becomes who, once initiated,
has zealously preserved the grace which comes
from the Mysteries*

[§ 1. Perfection in virtue resides in the will]

It has been mentioned what he becomes who has been initiated, and what way he must go if he is to preserve that which he has received from the Mysteries. It is fitting, then, to examine what he may become when he has preserved it, and what his character will be when he has added what is his to that which comes from God.

In our previous discussion we considered two things separately, the grace derived from the sacred rites, and zeal for preserving the gift on the part of those who have received it. These two combine in the life [in Christ]. It now remains for us to consider that life in its wholeness and to show both parts together, and how it is possible for all human virtue to concur with grace.

This, I think, we may achieve by examining the person who is compounded of both elements. If one wishes to expound the nature of this health, and the greatness of its benefit, one might well make it clear by considering him who most clearly enjoys it. By placing before our eyes him who has so lived, and looking at his excellence from every angle, let us discover his good health.

Nevertheless, we shall disregard his incidental ornaments, even if he be famous for working miracles and has received such grace. It is him alone and his proper ornament, the virtue of his soul, which we will examine. From the former we might infer that he is a good man; the latter alone would be sure proof of his worth. To have tested his character is to know the man himself.

Why then make conjectures and inferences when it is possible to perceive the very facts themselves? Even the power of working miracles would not be a sufficient proof of virtue. Neither do all who are virtuous have that power, nor are all who have it persons who practice virtue. Indeed, many who have achieved great things before God have displayed no such gifts while, on the contrary, some of the wicked have, at times, been able to do such things. It was not because of their merits that for those who call upon Christ nothing should be impossible; rather, it was in order that He whom they invoke should be manifested.

So it is for the sake of virtue that there are sacred rites and human efforts. As for miraculous powers, no one who had understanding ever found out how to acquire them. More than that, those saints who did not have them neither desired them nor sought for them. If we have them we may not even rejoice in them. "Do not rejoice," He says, "in this, that the spirits are subject to you; but rejoice that your names are written in heaven" (Lk. 10:20).

Since these powers neither produce virtue nor indicate its presence it is superfluous to take the trouble to seek for them. Not even if a man enjoys visions and obtains revelations and knows all mysteries (1 Cor. 13:2), will we pay attention to him or admire him. While such occasionally accompany those who live in Christ, they neither constitute nor effect that life, so that if one look to them alone it will not further him in virtue. This the blessed Paul shows as he writes to the Corinthians, "if I understand all mysteries and have all knowledge, but have not love, I am nothing,

and I am like a noisy gong or a clanging cymbal" (1 Cor.
13:2, 1).

Let us then leave other things aside and look at the will
of the soul itself. In this both the goodness and wickedness
of a man consist, his true health and his sickness, in short,
his life or death. The blessed life consists in this, that this
will should be good and tend to God alone.

[§ 2. How the Mysteries influence our wills
for goodness]

The effect, then, of the Mysteries and of meditation is
that a man's will should belong to Him alone who is truly
good. Nothing else may be seen as the goal of all God's
care for the human race. To it every promise of benefits
leads, as well as every threat of ill. To this end God built
the world for us and made laws. He favoured us with
countless blessings and deterred us with many penalties, in
order that He might turn us to Himself and persuade us
to desire Him and to love Him alone. This is evident in that
He demands from us, on whom He has bestowed His
benefits, this one tribute in return—that we should desire
goodness and be virtuous in our intention.

This is witnessed by all commandments, all good counsels,
in short, by every word which benefits man and leads to this.
As He does away with greed and punishes bodily lusts,
represses anger and casts out the memory of past ill, He
demands nothing but goodness and gentleness of will. In
addition, poverty of spirit, sorrow, showing mercy, meekness,
and each of the other things for which Christ called men
blessed if they practice them are all simply works of the will.
Further, it belongs to a right disposition that one assent to
right doctrines and believe concerning God that which is
true. In short, the whole law, says God, is given for the
sake of love. Love, however, is a virtue of the will.

When, therefore, after all His training and forethought
for the will, God demands from us its fruits, it is clear that
it is in the will that God sows all things and lays the

foundation for every ability and disposition for goodness. So it was for this reason that He gave us Baptism and initiated us in all the other rites, that He might create a good will in us. To this all the powers of the Mysteries and the new life contribute.

What then do the sacred rites achieve for us? They prepare us for the life to come. As Paul says, they are "powers of the age to come" (Heb. 6:5). But what is the one thing by which we are prepared? It is the keeping of the commandments of Him who is able to reward and to punish hereafter, for it is this which makes God dwell in us. "He who loves Me," Christ says, "will keep My commandments, and My Father will love him, and We will come and make our abode with him" (Jn. 14:23).

The keeping of His laws all depends on the will. There are rewards laid up for those who reverence the Lawgiver, and likewise penalties for those who ignore Him. To do this pertains to free will, for it belongs to the soul to be responsible in every way. Nobody would incur either reward or punishment for things which are entirely involuntary. Therefore, if we examine the will of him who lives in accordance with God we shall find the blessed life shining forth in it.

[§ 3. How pleasure and pain test the will]

In order that we may see the will in all its power let us examine it in its fullness, just as we might examine the strength of a body when it is most vigorous. ,

The fullness of will is pleasure and pain, pleasure as it aims for something, pain as it turns away from it. Accordingly, it appears from these what a person is, and they indicate the character of everyone and differentiate the wicked from the good. So men's life has two forms, that of the wicked who enjoy shameful and vain things, that of the good who enjoy good things. Again, the wicked are pained by the things that merely appear to be unpleasant, while the good are pained by the things which are truly bad. Not only wickedness and goodness, but also pleasantness and difficulty of life, prosperity and adversity, differ in this respect.

Is it not necessary, then, that those who are concerned about the blessed life contemplate these things, when it is possible thereby to learn both what that life is and in what its happiness consists? Since sorrow precedes joy, to the extent that joy is the fruit of sorrow (for He says, "those who mourn shall be comforted" [Mt. 5:4]) it is reasonable to begin our discussion with it. Further, to be vexed at what we ought, is to flee from evil, and so to rejoice aright means to pursue the good. Thus, in terms of time, joy follows upon sorrow, for it says, "depart from evil and do good" (Ps. 34:14, 1 Pet. 3:11).

In the preceding we have spoken of godly sorrow, and have discussed the things which, as we think of them, may move us to sorrow. But these considerations referred to other aspects and therefore could not embrace the whole of this emotion. We must therefore—and may God guide our discourse—observe what it is that gives pain to the virtuous man and in what way, as well as the other ways in which laudable grief differs from that which is wrong.

[§ 4. How true sorrow consists of hatred of sin]

It is clear to all that he who lives in God should grieve over the right things and in the right way. Yet since it is not plain to all for what things he must grieve and what is the fitting manner and suchlike, it will not be in vain that we consider them as far as we are able. Sorrow, therefore, depends on hating, and hating depends on regarding something as evil. We shun that which we consider to be evil, and suffer from the presence of things to which we are opposed and by which we are displeased. Accordingly, he who lives rightly and has laid hold of the true philosophy knows first what is truly evil, and then what he must hate, and suffers distress from the things by which he ought to be afflicted.

Let us therefore examine what is truly evil for man.

There are many things of all kinds which receive the name of evil. Some of these are troublesome to all men in general, while some of them are troublesome to some only; but there is nothing like wickedness of the soul and disease of the will. Some things are bad in themselves, such as the destructive influences of stars and disorders of seasons, barrenness of countries, rendings of the earth, earthquakes and pestilences, as well as poverty and disease, ill-treatment, imprisonment, and scourgings. But for man they are not at all evil. Such things harm him but outwardly and affect no more than his body and his possessions. The body is not the man to the extent that when it is sick he himself should be diseased. Even less need he be harmed in his humanity when those things have been taken away that must serve the body. Indeed, not even the opinion of the majority so convinces a man that he is worse when anyone thinks the worse of him. Were we to suppose this, a person might at the same time experience good fortune and ill, be both wicked and good, miserable and happy, since some have one opinion of him, and some the opposite.

If, however, true humanity consists of having will and reason, which no other beings here have in common with man, it is this which gives rise to virtue and wickedness alike. As for misfortune or prosperity, disease or health, living in distress or in enjoyment, the former would apply to those who have turned aside from the right way, while the other would belong to those who persist in the path of duty.

Since, then, perversion of reason is falsehood and perversion of will is wickedness, it remains for us to inquire by what sure proof we may recognize the aberration of each.

Of the many possibilities, the proof which is most reliable is the judgment of God Himself, for that which pleases Him is good and true, but that which He does not approve is worthless and false. The things which He expects man to learn are true, and that which He commands him to will is useful. As for the things which are contrary to them, they are full of deceit and wickedness. Some divine oracles came to men through human messengers. Of others

God Himself was the messenger, in that He clothed Himself with human nature and, as man, made known what was necessary by means of a voice proper to man. Is there anything better or truer than the precepts or teachings of which God Himself was the Lawgiver, Himself the spokesman, since He alone is good, He alone is the truth?

If, therefore, we need to learn what things cause pain to the true man by being a perversion of nature, we must take the opposite of God's laws. That which is truly evil opposes God's will. By being evil it is an object of hatred for him who cares for the good, and those who hate it wish that good may not come about when it is absent and suffer pain when it is present. By its presence evil causes the good pain, whether it is with them (as long as they have not taken leave of reason!) or with others for whom they pray. It is the good for which they pray for all men, by hastening to the divine loving-kindness and by desiring to see God's glory shining everywhere.

Thus sin alone is grievous to those who live in Christ, because it is evil while their character is virtuous, because it is contrary to God's laws, to whose will they strive to be united, and also, because for those who live in accordance with right reason it is most unsuitable to be vainly afflicted by anything else since they can derive the most useful fruits from pain. In other cases it makes no difference what suffering one undergoes—poverty, illness, and other such things will not be brought to cease merely by bewailing them.

In the case of evil of soul, suffering is the remedy. It averts future evil, causes present evil to cease, and is able to release us from punishment for past misdeeds. It was for this reason, I think, that the ability to suffer pain was given to our nature at the beginning, since it is not capable of helping us for anything else.

Now we do not venture to commit sin for no reason, but for the sake of gaining some reward of pleasure we barter away enjoyment of the good health of the soul. It is not for their own sake that we choose the ruin of the soul and the burning up of the mind! Once we know these things and repent of our sinful deeds we are distressed over them and despise the pleasure derived from them. We cast out the passion by means of its opposite, and show this by rejecting what we have accepted and by accepting what we have rejected. At the same time our suffering becomes the penalty which we pay for the sins which we have committed, and having been cleansed by it we need no further chastisement.

By this same means God from the beginning vindicates His laws when they have been violated, in that He punishes him who has broken them by means of pain and suffering. He would not have seen fit to exact this penalty were it not the opposite of the offence and capable of delivering from judgment. This was the method He Himself finally employed against sin when He entered into human nature. Because it was necessary to cast out sin from our nature it was by suffering that He cast it out.

So it is not only futile to suffer distress over something which pertains to the body, it is clearly harmful, for it means that we prefer something else to God. The final stage of such wickedness was the madness of Judas after he had sold his God and Saviour for a paltry sum of money. The seed of this state is to cease from the remembrance of Him. By loving something else in His place one is excluded from converse with Him. As this evil grows and forgetfulness of God occupies the soul, love for Him fades away, since that which is contrary to God increases by constant remembrance. Once affection has been extinguished, there straightway follows neglect of His commandments and breaking of His laws. Since, as He said, "he who loves Me will keep My commandments" (cf. Jn. 14:15), for those who tread under foot the laws of God nothing is unsuitable—even betraying the word of faith, if anything may be gained thereby.* As blessed Paul says, "some having swerved away from conscience have made shipwreck of their faith" (1 Tim. 1:6, 19). Of those who do not care for corresponding works

---

*Cabasilas may here be referring to Christians apostatizing to Islam in territories occupied by the Turks, in order to escape special taxes.

it is said that "their faith is dead" (Jas. 2:17). So it is hardly cause for wonder, if faith is readily destroyed.

There are three things which preserve our reverence for God: fear of the calamities which await the ungodly, the good hope of those who practice godliness, and love for God Himself and for goodness. None of these continues to affect the souls of those who have decided to break His laws. Just as those whose life is ordered by the laws of God increase in reverence for Him, so those who neglect His sayings soon lose this reverence, and have nothing in common with those who advance towards goodness. From him who has lost reverence for God all that might have availed to restrain wickedness has been removed. When one's reason, which might have introduced goodness, has been silenced by being frequently checked, it is not difficult for him to go on to the most desperate evils.

[§ 5. The Christian as the temple of God]

For these reasons the virtuous watch over this matter and resist the root of evils from the very beginning. They keep their heart for God alone, dedicating their memory to Him as a sacred precinct. They know that most men may not even touch sacred buildings, and that it is sacrilege to use vessels and hangings for consecrated things for any other purpose, and that no sacred thing is equal to a soul consecrated to God. Accordingly the house of God, more than anything else, must necessarily be out of bounds to those who buy and sell, and be far removed from the tables of the money changers and suchlike. If the house of prayer must be such, what must we think of him who prays, for whose sake it was necessary to cleanse that holy place from things that disturb?

Yet the name [i.e., 'house of prayer'] was not always applicable to the former Temple, nor was it always a house of prayer, since it sometimes lacked those who prayed. But the command of Paul bids Christians to apply themselves always to the presence of God, "praying without ceasing" (1 Thess. 5:17).

Let us consider this further. The Saviour who repelled other offences by means of words in one case employed both His tongue and His indignation, hand and whip alike, giving us occasion to consider how important He regards this matter. It was not so much because He wished to honour that Temple that He did these things, since He foresaw that it would be razed to the ground. Rather, He did this because He wanted to show how much He desires that each one of the faithful with whom He promised to abide should be freed from anxieties and cares, and at the same time how vehement was His passion and how great the need for constancy and sober reason. Above all, it is the Saviour Himself who takes the matter in hand. Unless we receive Him within ourselves it is impossible to cast out that which disturbs.

It was for these reasons that the [Mosaic] law decreed that sacrilege was punishable by death, and that the Holy of Holies had to have a veil. Uzzah died when he put an unhallowed hand to the tottering Ark (2 Sam. 6:6-7), and Uzziah acquired leprosy from the holy things (2 Chron. 26:16, 19). There are many such things which require that the baptized soul, like a pure and sacred precinct, should be inviolate for the true God.

[§ 6. The virtue of detachment]

It is most important, therefore, that those who live in Christ should keep the soul uncorrupted by worldly cares. Even if something enters the mind which seems to be important, it should not turn aside its reasoning, just as Peter, when he heard the Saviour's call, paid no heed at all to the things which he had in hand. In fact, all Christians too are being called with an unceasing call through the grace which has been impressed upon their souls by the Mysteries, which as Paul said, is "the Spirit of the Son of God in their hearts, crying, 'Abba! Father!' " Gal. 4:6).

In this way they despise all things in order that they may

always be able to follow Christ, for as it says, "it is not good to forsake the word of God and to serve tables" (Acts 6:2). They do this first because for them nothing comes before God, and second, because they expect to find all other things with Him, since He is the Dispenser of all good things. Indeed, those who seek first the kingdom of God have a promise from Him who cannot deceive that all other things will follow (Mt. 6:33).

For these reasons the Saviour withdraws from all earthly cares those who cleave to Him. He highly esteems this law, both in order that they may not be deprived of greater benefits, and also because it is in vain that they weary themselves with anxiety for the things He has already taken care of for them.

If, then, it is harmful to be anxious about these things, what shall we say about being distressed over them? Not only does it prevent the soul from being mindful of God, but it also entirely darkens and blinds reason, so that it readily proceeds thence to every kind of destruction. For if the mind, when it has been overcome by despondency, is then shaken by the perturbations which arise from this and so falls down, it is in a most wretched state. All too readily it surrenders its proper activity and dignity and that which is its own by nature, just as those who have been overcome by long drowsiness cast aside what they have in their hands. It readily yields to passion that which it ought to control, as though it were a slave. Thus nothing prevents the soul from dying after it has received countless blows, since there are, as David says, many who "war against it from on high" (Ps. 56:3 LXX), but no one who can help it. Therefore Paul says, "worldly grief produces death" (2 Cor. 7:10). As those who want their souls to survive consider these things, they not only shun grief, but avert the evil from afar by desisting from anxious care.

Even though many virtuous men have had to be busied with affairs because they were in charge of cities and estates, yet for that they were no more occupied with anxious cares, nor was their reason turned aside from its established course. We are anxious when it is uncertain whether we

shall receive what we desire and when irrational concern
has set in for the things which we want and for the means
which we employ for their attainment. It is these things
which can arouse anxiety and subject the soul to stress—
excessive desire for what we seek and uncertainty about the
attainment of that goal. But if we know nothing of the
objects of our desire or see no prospect of attaining them,
it is nothing grievous nor a source of anxiety. If we seek
what we love as though knowing for sure that we will not
receive it, no place is left for anxiety. For there is no care
nor fear when anxiety reaches its limit, but the passion is
simply that of grief for an evil as though it were already
present.

Since, however, none of the things which engender anxiety troubles the souls of those who live in Christ, they must
therefore be set free from the evils of anxiety, for they do
not cleave to any of the things of the present. In any work
that they perform for the need of the body they always
have some knowledge of the goal of their occupation, for
they pray that the end of their labours may be that which
pleases God, and they know very well that what is beyond
their prayers readily deceives.

These, then, are liable to suffer anxiety—those among
the poor who wish for luxury and seek to possess more than
is necessary for living, and those of the rich who care more
for money than for anything else. When the latter have it
they fear lest it should suddenly be lost, and are distressed
at their expenses, even when they spend money for what is
necessary for the body. They carry their self-love to such an
absurd length that they would rather have no benefit from
their treasures and always keep them hoarded up rather
than invest them for needed income, and that because they
are afraid of expending it in vain. They are unable to have
any confidence at all in the result of their labours, since they
have not set their hopes in the hand of God, which is firm
and enduring, but put their whole trust in themselves, their
reasonings and their actions, which as Solomon says, "are
worthless and likely to fail" (Wis. 9:14).

But those who hate all worldly delights and despise

all the things that are seen, use God's laws as a light for all their efforts for their own sake or for others. Since they do all things with the hope which they have in Him, that they will meet with that which will benefit them, what need is there for anxiety? Why should they lie awake because of things which they already know are in good order? Since they do not merely seek the end which follows on their efforts, but also that which will be useful to them, they do not look ahead with anxiety, but know well that they will obtain that for which they pray. They believe that what happens to those who love is of all things the most advantageous and that for which they have prayed. They are like travellers who, when they have found a guide who is well able to lead them to their destination, will have no fear of being led astray nor any anxiety about lodging for the night. In the same way those who have committed themselves to Him who is able to do all things have taken leave of all cares of self. Since they have entrusted their life and all its care to Him alone, their soul is free from anxiety. Thus, as they have regard for that which alone is truly good, they can be anxious for the things of the Lord. So they fear and are anxious, if need be, only for that which pleases Him.

In this way, then, they have become useful not only to themselves, but to others as well. Well might one marvel at God's kindness in this, that while no one may be cured of illness by another taking his medicine, yet the sufferings of others might avail to set one free from judgment.

[§ 7. How we ought to sorrow over sin]

From what has been said it is clear what it is that troubles those who wish to live in Christ. It remains for us to discuss in what way this is so, and for what reasons.

It is not for the same reasons that all feel grief over sin. Some are moved to bewail it because of vainglory, since, while they have the highest opinion of themselves they are disappointed in their expectations. In other cases, I think, it is the loss of rewards which is painful. For most people it is the fear of punishment which makes it unbearable to transgress God's law; in the case of the very best it is love for the Lawgiver Himself.

Pre-eminent among those who live virtuously are those who are moved to strive for virtue, not by fear of evils or hope of reward, but by love of God alone. Similarly, of those who lament their sins the best are those whose sorrow is kindled by love for God. Others move themselves to sorrow and of themselves attain to it and mourn because of self-love; but the former are moved to sorrow by God Himself. Accordingly, since the motion must be congruous with the Mover, this sorrow is as much superior to the other as its Cause is the greater, just as the best path of an arrow, that which goes straight to the target, comes from the hands of such as are skilled in archery.

Now it is necessary not only to know for what we ought to feel grief, and how we ought to do so, but also how much. It is possible to be distressed at one's sins, but less than is fitting, and also to indulge in excessive sorrow. Those who are moved by the previously mentioned considerations to bewail their sins will know the due measure of tears.

In the case of bodily illness, as long as a member is diseased, there is either nothing at all that can take the place of the flesh which has been destroyed, or else it is unnaturally swollen and out of due proportion. But when nature has been restored to its order and is free of disease, the limb straightway returns to its due proportion and is at rest without adding anything more than has been removed. The same might apply to ailments of the soul. All such things as sorrow, distress, and tears for our offences have for their aim the removal of sin and the restoration of whatever good the soul has lost. Thus, since it is that sorrow which proceeds from divine love which alone is healthy, it alone is agreeable to reason. It only, rather than the other, knows the due measure. In this case, even if men transgress they neither turn elsewhere nor change their course. If the love of God remains in them they do not lose knowledge of where to go or where to find rest.

[§ 8. Such godly sorrow springs
from the love of God]

To walk straight to God is to walk in love. This is the
way of the undefiled who, as the Psalmist says, "seek Him
with their whole heart" (Ps. 119:2), thereby showing what
is the desire which has been enjoined upon us. Those who
"walk in the law of the Lord" (Ps. 119:1) are those who
live in love, the commandment on which the whole law
depends (Mt. 22:40). They do so in order that they may
straightway strip themselves of all sin, which alone obscures
the vision of the soul. Nothing then impedes them from
looking towards right reason even in their desires and from
knowing clearly how much they ought to lament.

As I have said before, the aim of human virtue is to share
in God's will, while the aim of wickedness is the opposite.
The former means that man attains his goal, the latter that
he falls short of it.* When those who live philosophically
for reward are virtuous, it is not because they love virtue
for itself. When they fall from it they do not deplore sin
on its own account. They practice virtue because they desire
rewards and shun sin because of its penalty. Thus it is not
the substance of sin, so to speak, which they really hate,
and even when they have ceased from actively sinning they do
not really flee from it in the disposition of their will. Just as
he who hates wicked men cannot properly be called a hater
of mankind, so to feel abhorrence of sin merely because it
brings punishment on its perpetrator rather than because it
conflicts with God's laws is not to shun wickedness itself but
merely to flee from its punishment. It is quite clear that were
it possible to sin without peril to oneself such men would
not flee from evil.

But those whose affection for God exalts them to a
philosophical life honour the law because they love its
Giver. When they have offended God they condemn themselves and blame themselves for the sin itself and bewail

---

*The Greek verb means both "to sin" and "to miss the goal."

it, not because they were cheated of the rewards of virtue but because their will was not in harmony with God.

When, therefore, the former have repented of their offences they are not completely pure from evil in their souls. They still must seek the due measure of wretchedness and lamentation and labours for their offences, while the latter, since they have cast out all disease, will be self-sufficient in this regard. Since sin has two aspects* they flee from both. They have ceased from sinful action by penitence. Evil passion does not persist in them, nor any disposition to sin, since their passion for goodness and for God cleaves to their souls and does not admit them.

[§ 9. The Christian's joy]

So much, then, for sorrow. Joy befits us when the things which we love are present with us, and also when we hope for them. For "we rejoice in hope" (Rom. 12:12), as Paul says, since love and hope have the same objects. Indeed, we have joy in ourselves to the extent that we love.

Now there are those who are pleasant in themselves, since they themselves are good in character, and are so in the view of kindly friends. So the virtuous man, since he realizes that goodness alone is worthy of love, for its sake has joy in himself. For its sake also he has joy in others, whether it is because they are of like character, or because they assist him in goodness. In addition to this, the good man rejoices in the good of others, for this too is the object of his prayers and desires, that another should enjoy good fortune.

This is the most generous form of pleasure, that one should share in the pleasure of another soul, and not merely desire for oneself and one's own benefit, nor take pride merely in that which is one's own, nor love one's own gain alone, but consider oneself rewarded by the triumph of others. In this, man goes beyond his nature and becomes

---

*I.e., act and motive.

like God who is the common good of all. Further, in this way it becomes evident that a man loves goodness for its own sake and not for its usefulness to himself when he is no less pleased at seeing others have it.

So it belongs to good men to desire the good of all men and to rejoice at their prosperity. One might well regard this as the sign that they are perfectly virtuous, just as the fruit which the tree brings forth clearly shows that it is healthy. Nature would not suffer a plant to bring forth fruit before it has reached maturity in itself, nor would any man be useful to others without first having become useful to himself. He is intimate with himself before he has intimacy with others; he is familar with himself and deals with himself before all others, and desires and prays for that which is useful to himself. What, then, prevents him from first profiting himself if, on the one hand, he rejoices in that which is good, and nature on the other hand turns him first to himself and to forethought for himself, just as it does for all other beings? In short, he exists for himself, and is good for himself first of all. That each man should be himself is the first and most general desire of all men.

It is evident, therefore, that if a man loves the prosperity of others and rejoices when they attain it he is not himself deprived of it nor deficient in it. He does not show concern for others by neglecting himself and his own interests and needs. How could one wish to see in the hands of others that which he knows his own house lacks?

Even though some of those who are indifferent towards goodness and virtue assume the mask of the best qualities, pretend virtue, and seek to lead others in the things of which they are wholly ignorant, they do not make the effort for the sake of virtue and goodness, but merely to gain reputation and false glory. Right reason shows that it is impossible for those who try to do this to become perfectly virtuous! Perfect virtue is possible only for those who have been set free from all envy and malice, and who display genuine and perfect love towards their fellow men, which is the attainment of the highest philosophy.

Therefore, to partake of this pleasure it is necessary to be the best and wisest of all men, while those who are best and wisest must have part in this pleasure. Consequently, those who partake of goodness must display the nature of that goodness in the soul, for it is the nature of goodness to be diffused and shared. Just as all things aim at it, so its nature is to spread abroad to all things. If it did not impart itself to all, all things would not seek to obtain it, for how would it be reasonable if the desire which is of all most general were in vain?

Accordingly, the very principle of virtue demands that the good man devote himself to all men even as to himself, and that his soul experience feelings such as distress and joy no less with regard to the affairs of others than to his own. Furthermore, it is his love for God which leads him to this joy, for he who loves must find joy not only in the one whom he loves, but also in the same things which give joy to the object of his love.

[§ 10. The source of our joy is love for God]

We have now come to the most perfect and pure joy. Since he who lives in God loves Him above all things and rejoices with the joy that befits so great an affection, so we must examine its nature and characteristics more closely. Firstly, he who lives thus does not claim to be the source of his own joy. Such a thought does not belong to one who truly loves God Himself, but rather to one who loves himself and looks on himself as the end of all that he does. Yet how would a grateful man fail to love Him who is his Benefactor above all others? How would a just man give less love to Him who most of all deserves to be loved? How would a wise man prefer anything to the final goal?

Since it is reasonable that the grateful man should be righteous and wise as well, he must love God and rejoice in Him in the most perfect way. Accordingly, his joy must be constant, stable, and exceeding great and wondrous. It must be constant, since he is at all times amid things which belong to Him whom he desires and constantly encounters them, whether they serve his physical needs or form the subjects of his thoughts—things by which he subsists, lives, survives, and is engaged in activity, and in any way feels and acts. All these things he knows to be God's works and always present with him. Accordingly they all keep him mindful of God, they all preserve love from being quenched, and all delight him. He will neither neglect himself nor cease from being conscious of himself, nor will anything be capable of interrupting this joy. For when we are in the company of those whom we love it is not only in them that we rejoice, but also in their deeds and in everything that we in any way have in common with them.

Further, they too have a constant joy who derive much pleasure from themselves and are able to find contentment by themselves. He who has much pleasure will neither cease from it, nor will that which is pleasant cease from giving him pleasure. When his pleasure is such he will not be able to reproach either his passion or himself, since it cannot be called unreasonable or unjustified, but is actually in accord with reason. He has that which is pleasant, and it is impossible to fear for it or to nourish any suspicion that it has any "variation or shadow of change" (Jas. 1:17).

One might be able to perceive how great that pleasure is if one were to look at that which itself causes the delight, for the joy must be in proportion to the greatness of its source. So, as nothing is comparable to God, men have nothing like the joy that is derived from Him, since the power of the desire is in keeping with its object. When that which is desired is so great, the power of the desire is not inferior and insufficient for such an abundance of goodness, but is in proportion to that infinity and is disposed accordingly. Though our desire is limited by being in proportion to human nature, yet among created things we see nothing which is adequate to Him, since all things are inferior to Him and fall below Him. Were we even to attain to all good things in existence, we would still look beyond them and seek what we do not have while ignoring what we have. Nothing created will cause our desire to be

at rest or make us perfectly content or give full scope for
the soul's faculty of joy.

It is thus clear that while man's ability to desire is limited,
it has been created with infinite good as its object. Man's
nature is limited, but not its activity and its desire. So we
know plainly that while the whole life of the soul belongs to
a limited being, yet it has no end. The reason for this is
that God has created not only the life of the soul, but also
its joy and all that is ours, with a view to Himself. The life
is immortal in order that we, by death, may live with Him;
the joy is unbounded in order that we may enjoy Him with
perfect pleasure.

Since then these two have joined in one, endless goodness
without limit, and fulfilment of infinite desire, how great the
matter for pleasure! Yet we cannot experience so great an
overflowing of joy merely by rejoicing in the attainment of
the object of our desire. Our joy would then be merely in
proportion to the attainment of its object, our pleasure limited
by the extent that we failed to attain it. Actually, there is
joy because of all the blessedness which is in God. Whatever
we know of God leads to pleasure, since the object that we
seek is not ourselves, but God. If the goal of our lives is not
merely self, our wills will not be directed merely towards
our own good, but towards Him. We would rejoice at divine
benefits not because we ourselves enjoy them, but to the
extent that God is in them. We would leave self behind and
hasten to God with all our will, and forget our own property
and look with eagerness to these riches. When we would see
the good fortune of another we should esteem it as though
it were our own possession, nor think ourselves unfortunate
because of it, but know that on its account we are rich and
blessed.

The power of love, then, is able to make those who love
partake of that which belongs to the objects of their love.
Since in the case of the saints all the power of their will
and desire spends itself for God, they regard Him alone as
their proper good. The body cannot delight them, nor can
the soul nor its good things, nor yet anything else that is
innate and proper to nature, since they are to love none of

these things for its own sake. They have, as it were, once for all gone out of themselves and removed their life and all their desire elsewhere, and so lost knowledge of self.

This is nothing incredible; for human love moves men to despise their possessions and their bodies. You may see how those who love madly pay no attention to their health when they themselves are healthy and they see their friends suffer ill health; nor do they heed their own illness when they themselves are sick and their friends are in health. Many would gladly die to help their friends and would rather give up their own bodies than to see them be destroyed. As for love towards God, it is so much greater than love for men since there is such a great difference between the objects of love.

[§ 11. How the love of God issues in self-giving and self-surrender]

What, then, is left that we may spend it for Him? Or what greater thing shall we give Him when he who is constrained by love despise his very soul? It is not he who has slain the body who truly ignores the soul, but he who surrenders the soul and its good things as well. Just as the depraved man spends himself completely for the pleasures of the body, so he who loves God surrenders himself by applying all the energy and desire of the soul to God without anything left over for the soul itself. Even though he employs reason in order to be healthy, yet it is not for the sake of seeking the soul and its benefits, but for the sake of loving God and caring for His laws in order that he may be saved. It is like taking care of a tool for the sake of the work, as when the wheelwright uses his tool for a wagon, it is the wagon with which he is concerned rather than the tool itself.

In this way too we may make it clear. What is it that persuades us to cling to the soul and greatly love it? It is nothing else than the will to exist. We wish to exist because we wish to be happy, for one cannot bear to exist and be in misery. For this reason many have done away with themselves; and, as the Saviour says, "it would have been better for him if he had not been born" (Mt. 26:24). Since to be truly happy is nothing else than to love God, it is altogether clear that to love God is also to love the soul itself. Since most men do not know whence they may obtain happiness, they each love different things. By turning aside from the straight course that leads to the goal they often choose things which make them worse, and so neither honour the soul as they ought, nor disregard it according to reason.

The virtuous, however, order themselves in relation to God as knowing where to seek their being and how they are to be useful to themselves. They look on God alone as the object of love and love Him alone for His own sake, and for His sake they love their souls, existence, and all other things as well. So when they love the soul it is not the real object of their love, but rather God, for whose sake they love it.

If we love the soul as though it were something of our own, it is the Saviour who will belong to us more than the soul itself. Those who pay heed to this throughout life know that the Saviour has become akin to them in every way, and because of Him the soul and existence itself are dear and congenial. A man is anxious for himself if he suffers from conflicts, and he will not be able to find serenity unless he finds God.

In addition, those who live in Christ, whom we must regard as having a right judgment of things, do not withhold from Him that which befits Him. This is the case if we love Him who is perfectly good with our love. Our love would be imperfect if we loved something else beside Him and divided our affection, since the law also says, "you shall love God with all your soul and with all your mind" (Deut. 6:5, cf. Mk. 12:30). Since, therefore, those who live in Christ decide to refer all their love to God and to leave no part of it either for other things or for themselves, they have forsaken themselves and all things in their purpose, for it is love which in every case joins together. Thus, by removing themselves from all things they live for God alone. Him alone they love, in Him alone they rejoice.

[§ 12. How self-surrender leads to joy]

As for the things which are most of all our own, we wish to be with them and enjoy them, not so much because they are our own, but rather because we love them. Even were this not so, mere possession does not avail to attach us to them or cause us to enjoy them. Many things which are our own distress us, and we have things for which we reproach ourselves. There are even some who obviously hate themselves and wish to run away and die. Some have actually perpetrated this and have departed before their allotted time by forcing death on themselves by sword or by hanging. Accordingly it is clear that it is love which prompts us to be with all the things with which we live and which we enjoy, and to enjoy their use, such as the soul, our intimate friends, and our very selves. If one therefore desires the good of others and loves it no less than his own good he must agree with them in will and rejoice with them in their good fortune no less than he does with himself in his own.

Therefore, even though the nature of him who loves God has not been transformed into the divine nature, yet when his will and love have been diverted from that which is his own, nothing prevents the joy which is in him from being as complete as though he had been transformed. Even though he still bears human nature and does not naturally live with things divine as though they were his own, yet at them he directs his whole will, which determines how he is to find joy and causes one pleasure or the other to prevail. Just as he who loves himself is happy with what he has because he considers it to be good, so those who love God alone derive pleasure for themselves from His benefits. They are rich in the things which are His, they boast of them and take pride in His glory. They are rewarded when He is worshipped and are exalted when He is honoured.

But those who live for themselves, even when they derive

joy from the things which are truly good, are unable to
reap unmixed pleasure. While they rejoice in the good things
which are at hand, so naturally evils, whether present or
absent, cause them distress. Those who have transferred their
life to God have unalloyed pleasure and no sadness at all.
While there are many things which may harm them, there
is nothing that distresses them, for there is nothing unpleasant with God, for whom they live. They have no perception of things present, even if among them something is
capable of causing them pain. The principle of perfect love
does not permit them to seek their own, for as it is said,
"love seeks not its own" (1 Cor. 13:5). Rather, they love
because He whom they love is blessed, and they are possessed
by a strange and extraordinary passion. Though they are earth
and ashes, yet they exchange what is their own for the things
of God and become like Him, just as if poor and wretched
men were to rush into a royal palace and cast away all their
own poverty and be clothed with all the splendour that
befits the place.

For this reason, too, I think that they are spoken of as
"violent men" who "take the kingdom of heaven by force"
(Mt. 11:12) since they do not wait for those who will
give it to them nor look for those who will choose them,
but occupy the throne of their own accord and put the crown
on themselves on their own initiative. Even though they
take it, yet they do not consider themselves to be fortunate
thereby, nor is it from this that they derive pleasure, but
rather because they know that the kingdom consists in Him
whom they love. They have joy, not because He shares His
benefits with them, but because He is in the benefits, since
they have Him with them and enjoy His benevolence. Hence,
even if they were given no share in the kingdom, and the
object of their love had not made them partakers of His
blessedness, yet having Him they would be no less fortunate
and reign as kings and be rewarded and enjoy that kingdom.
Thus they may fitly be styled "robbers" and violent possessors
of divine benefits for the reason that they have thrust themselves inside in order to enjoy them. These are they who

hate their souls and lose them (cf. Mt. 16:25) and in place of them receive the Master of souls.

What, then, is greater or more constant than this joy? In the case of those who find joy in themselves it is not unexpected that they should lose that which pleases them, for there is no permanent good in anything present. Accordingly, their joy in the things which they enjoy is no greater than their distress over the riches for which they tremble with fear. But in the case of the saints the treasure of good things is inviolate and pleasure is unalloyed with sorrow, and there is no fear for something which is stable and firm.

Those whose joy is in themselves rightly suspect that their joy may lead them into arrogance since they look so much at themselves, and this cuts off the greater part of their pleasure. Those who attribute all power to God and boast in Him are not at all so troubled, since they do not look back on themselves. Theirs is thus a joy not merely according to human ability as is common to men, but one that is supernatural and divine. It is as if a man were to exchange one house for another and acquire one that is better, and in anticipation derive pleasure from the latter house instead of from the former. Similarly, were he by some means to obtain a better body by getting rid of his present one, he would exchange the enjoyment proper to it and find as much more pleasure as the body he would be using would be better. Therefore, when one casts away not merely one's body and one's house, but one's very self and receives God as reward, God will take the place of body, soul, family, friends, and all that one has. So the pleasure this brings must exceed all human pleasure, and one will receive therefrom that enjoyment which is appropriate to the divine blessedness and befits such a transformation.

For this reason too, it is said that the blessed rejoice with the joy of Christ, for that in which He rejoices gives them joy as well. He rejoices in Himself, so it follows that those who are able to share in His joy will enjoy the same degree of pleasure. This we may learn for certain not merely by inference and reasoning, but from the clear words of the

Saviour. When He had instituted the laws of love He also
exhorted His disciples to keep their affection for Him un-
changed to the end. "These things have I spoken to you,"
He said, "that My joy may abide in you, and that your joy
may be full" (Jn. 15:11). By this He meant, "therefore I
command you to love, that when love has made all that is
Mine yours also, you may find joy with the same pleasure
which is in Me and in Mine." It is said, "for you have
died, and your life is hid with Christ in God" (Col. 3:3).
The same is true of joy and all other things, and so there
is nothing human in them.

[§ 13. How love for God leads to forgetfulness of self]

The blessed Paul makes all things clear in a brief saying,
"you are not your own, you were bought with a price"
(1 Cor. 6:19-20). He who has been purchased does not
regard himself but Him who has purchased him, and lives
according to His will. In the case of men, the slave is bound
to the wish of his master, but only in body; in his mind and
reason he is free and can use them as he pleases. But in the
case of him whom Christ has bought it is impossible for him
to be his own. Since no man has ever bought a complete
man, and there is no price for which it is possible to purchase
a human soul, so no one has ever set a man free or enslaved
him save with respect to his body. The Saviour, however,
has bought the whole of man. While men merely spend
money to buy a slave, He spent Himself. For our freedom
He surrendered body and soul by causing the one to die and
by depriving the other of its own body. His body suffered
pains by being wounded; His soul was troubled, and that
not merely when the body was slain, but even before it was
wounded, as He said, "My soul is very sorrowful, even to
death" (Mt. 28:38).

So, by giving Himself completely, He purchased the
whole man. Therefore He has purchased the will too, and it
especially. In other respects He was our Master and had

control over our whole nature; but it was by our will that we escaped from His service, and He did everything to capture it. Because of the fact that it was our will which He was seeking, He did no violence to it nor took it captive, but He bought it. Thus, of those who have been bought, no one will do right by using his will for himself, but will commit an injustice to Him who has bought him by depriving Him of His possession. It is by self-will and by rejoicing in that which is one's own that one would use one's will for oneself.

So it remains that none of the virtuous and righteous loves himself, but only Him who has bought him. It must be that at least some, if not all, of those who have been purchased should be thus disposed. How could it be reasonable for such an awesome purchase to have been made in vain? For those who love only Him it follows that they should enjoy all pleasure unalloyed with trouble, since He whom they love does nothing contrary to their desires. They are moved with an exceedingly great and supernatural divine power of joy, and this power finds complete fulfilment, and that which delights them surpasses every abundance of grace.

Furthermore, just as he who is a slave of men inevitably has grief, so he who is Christ's slave is bound to have joy. Since the former no longer gives way to his own will but to the will of him who has bought him, he undergoes labours and pains as he follows him who is responsible for his grief and pains. But how will the latter suffer distress when he is led on by true joy? He who spent money for a slave did not spend it with the aim of conferring benefits on him whom he has bought, but rather that he himself might derive benefit by exploiting his labours. The slave is, as it were, being spent for the profit of those who have acquired him and through whom he suffers misery, and gathers pleasures for them while he himself is subject to constant sorrows.

In the case of the slaves of Christ the opposite is true, for everything has been accomplished for their benefit. He paid the ransom, not in order to enjoy anything from those who have been ransomed, but in order that what is His might belong to them, and that the Master and His labours

might profit the slaves, and that he who has been purchased
might himself wholly possess Him who has purchased him.
For this cause those who have not leaped away from this
servitude but have preferred His bonds to every kind of
freedom must have joy, since they have exchanged poverty for
riches, a prison for a kingdom, final disgrace for the highest
glory. That which, among men, masters may lawfully do
to their slaves, the slaves may here do to their common
Master because of His loving-kindness. Among men the
law makes the masters lords over their slaves and possessions
unless they renounce their domination or release them from
servitude. In this case, however, the slaves possess their own
Master and inherit that which is His when they love His
yoke and regard themselves as bound by His act of purchase.
This is why Paul commanded, "Rejoice in the Lord" (Phil.
4:4), meaning by "the Lord" Him who has purchased them.

The Saviour points out to us a yet more evident cause for
joy when He calls him who shares in His joy a "good
servant" and Himself "Master" when He says, "enter, O
good servant, into the joy of your Master" (Mt. 25:21).
That is, "because you remained a servant and did not tear
up the bill of your purchase, receive the joy of Him who
has bought you." It is the same joy, not only because that
which pleases is the same, but also because it is the same
kind of sentiment. For just as He "did not please Himself"
(Rom. 15:3) but lived and died for His servants, and was
born at the beginning and returned to Himself and possesses
the Father's throne where He is seated for us and is an
Advocate with Him for ever (cf. 1 Jn. 2:1), so He belongs
to the servants for whom their Master has become dearer than
their very souls and who, without turning to themselves, love
Him alone.

[§ 14. Examples of selfless service for Christ]

Such was John the Baptist. When he was tested by Christ's
appearing he was so far from taking offence that it was
he who proclaimed Him to those knew Him not (cf. Jn.

3:29, 30). Nothing was more pleasing to him than that saying by which he detracted from his own glory. He thought it right that Christ should attract attention to Himself and assume the leadership of the whole human race, and that all should turn their minds to Him as the bride does to the bridegroom. He himself preferred to stand by and hear Him speak, and to enjoy with all eagerness the voice of the Beloved (Jn. 3:29).

As Paul sought the things of Christ he not only despised himself but even abandoned himself. As far as he was able, he even rushed into hell, for he prayed that he might suffer this (Rom. 9:3) [for the conversion of the Jews], and was as it were an enigma. Because he greatly loved Him whom he loved, he desired to suffer loss (cf. 1 Cor. 3:15, Phil. 3:8). It seems that not only did his love inflame him more vehemently than hell, but even that it prevailed over the joy that was in the converse with Him whom he loved. Just as he persuaded men to think lightly of hell, so he readily taught them to disregard joy, even though he already had a clear experience of it and had tasted its beauty. Since, however, it pertained to Christ and His honour to be with Him, to live with Him, and reign with Him, Paul not only did not seek his own glory rather than Christ's, but was anxious to prefer it over his own. When, therefore, he desired, it was for Christ's sake and not his own. Had it been necessary to flee for His sake, he would have taken to flight (cf. Acts 9:25, 2 Cor. 11:33). If, then, it was not for his own sake that he wished for the only Object of desire, what then in the case of all other objects? If he sought Him for whom he did all things, endured all things, without regard for himself, he would scarcely have sought any of the other things which he despised in order that he himself might derive enjoyment. Accordingly it is clear that he wholly fled from himself and cast out all his own will, and that his will was active only in relation to Christ. Since with Christ there was nothing undesirable or repugnant to his will, it follows that his was a wondrous pleasure which was always present and with which he always lived, and that no unpleasantness prevailed over that soul.

While there were things over which Paul was in travail
and anguish, yet that which caused distress did not prevail
over the pleasure, nor did it drive away anything that
belonged to it. Even his apparent faintness of heart was
fulness of joy, for the sorrow was the fruit of love and
magnanimity and it brought into his heart nothing that was
bitter, violent, or mean. It is evident that he himself was
always full of joy since he exhorted others to be always
joyful, for he says, "rejoice in the Lord always; again I will
say, rejoice" (Phil. 4:4). He would not have enjoined on
others what he himself had not first displayed in deeds.

[§ 15. The life in Christ may be summed up by love and joy]

Such is the life of the saints and in this way it is blessed.
As is fitting, we call those blessed who by hope and faith
reap the fruit of blessedness. After they have departed, it
is so much better as the partaking of the realities themselves
is more perfect than hoping for them, and the pure contemplation of the good is more perfect than faith.

The good of this life is, in part, the Spirit of adoption
from God, from whence comes that perfect love in accordance
with which the blessed life is lived. The Spirit permits us to
receive the Mysteries of Christ, and as it is said, to those
who receive Him "He gave power to become children of
God" (Jn. 1:12). It is to the children that the perfect love
belongs from which "all fear has been driven away" (cf. 1
Jn. 4:12). He who loves in that way cannot fear either the
loss of rewards or the incurring of penalties, for the latter
fear belongs to slaves, the former to hirelings. To love purely
in this manner belongs to sons alone.

Thus grace implants true love into the souls of those who
have been initiated. Those who seek to learn may know what
it effects and what experience it brings. Generally speaking,
it imparts the perception of divine benefits, and by the experience of great things it inspires hope of things yet greater,
and from things already present it inspires faith concerning
things which do not yet appear.

It is in our power to persevere in that love, for it is not enough to love and experience its passion, but it is necessary as well to persevere in it and to add fuel to the fire so that it may persist, for this is to abide in love. All blessedness consists in this. To abide in love is to abide in God, and for him who abides in Him to possess Him, for it says, "he who abides in love abides in God, and God abides in him" (1 Jn. 4:16). This happens when we have love firmly fixed in the will, and arrive at that through the commandments and keep the laws of Him whom we love. It is by actions that the soul is disposed towards one habit or the other, so that men may partake of goodness or wickedness, just as in the case of crafts we acquire skills and learn them by becoming accustomed to their exercise. God's laws which apply to human activities and determine and order them towards Him alone impart the appropriate habit to those who act rightly, which is to will that which pleases the Lawgiver and to subject all our will to Him alone and to will nothing apart from Him. This alone is to know how to love properly, and for this reason the Saviour says, "if you keep My commandments, you will abide in My love" (Jn. 15:10).

The effect of this love is the blessed life. As it draws the will together from all sides and leads it away from all other things, and even from him who wills, it commends it to Christ alone. All that is ours follows the will and moves where it is borne by it, whether it is the effort of the body or the movement of reason, any action or anything else that is proper to man. In short, it is the will which, as far as we are concerned, leads us and carries us. If it is in some way restrained all things are impeded thereby, and when anything gains possession of the will it has control over the whole mind.

Therefore, for those whose will is altogether captured by the will of Christ and belongs to Him entirely, He is all that they desire and love and seek. All their being and life is with Him, since their very will cannot live and be active unless it abides in Christ where all good resides. Just as it is impossible for the eye to fulfill its function without making use of light since it is the light alone which enables it to

see, so in the case of the will it is able to function for goodness only. Since He, then, is the Dispenser of all good things,
if we fail to set all our will on Him, or our will in part
falls short of this treasure, it is idle and dead. As He says,
"if a man does not abide in Me, he is cast forth as a branch
and withers; and the branches are gathered, thrown into the
fire, and burned" (Jn. 15:6).

If, then, to imitate Christ and to live according to Him
is to live in Christ, this life is the effect of the will when it
obeys God's purposes. Just as Christ subjected His human
will to His divine will in order that He might leave us
an example of the right life, so He did not refuse death on
behalf of the world when it was necessary to die. But before
the time came He prayed that it might not happen, showing
that He did not please Himself by the things which He
suffered, but as Paul says, "He became obedient" (Phil.
2:8) and went to the cross, not as though He had one will,
or one compounded out of two, but rather the agreement of
two wills.

Thus it appears in all things that the blessed life consists
in the perfection of the will in the present life. Since man
possesses mind and will, it is necessary that he who is to be
completely blessed should agree with God in both these
things and be conjoined to Him—by his mind in pure contemplation of Him, by his will by perfectly loving Him.
Yet it happens that none of those who live in a corruptible
body enjoy happiness in both these respects. It is only the life
which is freed from corruption which admits of such men.

In the present life those who are blessed are perfect in
relation to God in respect of their will, but not yet with
respect to the activity of their mind. One may find perfect
love in them, but by no means pure contemplation of God.
If, however, that which is in the future is present with them
while they yet live in the body, they already experience the
prize, yet not continually or perfectly, since this life does
not permit it. For this cause Paul says, "we rejoice in hope"
(Rom. 12:12), and "we walk by faith, not by sight" (2 Cor.
5:7), and "we know in part" (1 Cor. 13:9). Even though
he had seen Christ (1 Cor. 9:1, 15:8), yet he did not enjoy

this vision at all times. For "always" looks to the future only, and this he himself showed when he spoke of Christ's presence, saying, "and so shall we always be with the Lord" (1 Thess. 4:17). Thus, anyone who is in Christ and has received eternal life has it through his will, and through love he will arrive at the ineffable joy. He has the pure vision of the mind in store for the future while faith leads him on to love. This the blessed Peter shows, saying, "though you do not see Him you believe in Him and rejoice with unutterable and exalted joy" (1 Pet. 1:8).

In this love and joy the blessed life consists. This life is partly hidden—according to that word of Paul which says, "your life is hid" (Col. 3:3)—and partly revealed. As the Lord says, "the wind blows where it wills, and you hear the sound of it, but you do not know whence it comes or whither it goes; so it is with every one who is born of the Spirit" (Jn. 3:8). That which concerns the very grace which generates and forms, the nature of this life and the manner in which it is refashioned, is invisible. What becomes apparent to those who partake of it is an ineffable love for God and the joy which is in Him. These very things are apparent and indicate the invisible grace. In the first place they are the fruit of that grace, for it says, "the fruit of the Spirit is love, joy" (Gal. 5:22), and "the tree is known by its fruit" (Mt. 12:33). Then, since the grace is the Spirit of adoption, the love bears witness of this kinship to the sons of God, because it contains nothing mercenary nor servile.

Thus it was that Solomon also considered the great love of the woman for the living child sufficient proof that she had given birth to it. Accordingly it is not unreasonable that we by this sign discern the sons of the living God. Just as her affection for the living child and her concern for it clearly showed that she had no kinship with the child that had died, so is it the case of the sons of God that their reverence for the living God and affection for Him clearly prove that they have not sprung from dead forefathers but from Himself. The Saviour did not permit those who so live in Him even to bury their dead, for He said, "leave the dead to bury their own dead" (Mt. 8:22).

Nor is it by the mere fact of loving that they confirm
their sonship, by cleaving to God and loving Him as their
Father, but also by becoming like Him through love. They
are filled with love, but "God is love" (1 Jn. 4:16), and
they live for love. It is those in whom this noble passion is
nourished who truly live, just as all things are dead for those
in whom it is absent. Therefore because they are sons they
honour the Father by their actions. By being themselves alive
they proclaim the living God by whom they have been
begotten. By the "newness of life" (Rom. 6:4) in which
they, in accordance with Paul's word, are walking, they put
their trust in Him and "glorify the Father who is in heaven"
(Mt. 5:16). Thus they are ineffably generated by His loving-
kindness. As is fitting, "He is not God of the dead, but of
the living" (Mt. 22:32), because with them He finds His
proper glory. Accordingly He also said to the wicked, "if
I am God, where is My glory?" (Mal. 1:6). This David
also showed by saying, "the dead shall not praise Thee, O
Lord, but we who live" (cf. Ps. 115:17-18 LXX).

Such is the life in Christ, concealed, and thus made
manifest by the light of good works, which is love. In love
the brightness of all virtue consists and, as far as human
effort is concerned, it constitutes the life in Christ. Accordingly one would not err by calling it life, for it is union
with God. This union is life, just as we know that death is
separation from God. For this reason Christ says, "His commandment is eternal life" (Jn. 12:50). Speaking of love
the Saviour also says, "the words that I speak to you
are spirit and life" (Jn. 6:63), of which love is the sum,
and "he who abides in love abides in God and God in him"
(1 Jn. 4:16), which is the same as abiding in life and life in
Him, for He says, "I am the life" (Jn. 11:25, 14:6).

If life is also the power that moves the things which
live, what is it that moves those men who truly live, whose
God is God, who "is not the God of the dead, but of the
living" (Mk. 12:27)? You will find that it is nothing but
love itself, which not only leads and moves them, but also
readily brings them out of themselves, and is thus more
capable than any life of having the effect that life may the

more prevail! It persuades men to despise life, not merely that which is transitory, but even that which stands firm.

What then may life be more fittingly called than love? For that which alone survives and does not allow the living to die when all things have been taken away is life—and such is love. When all things have passed away in the age to come as Paul says (1 Cor. 13:8, 10), love remains, and it alone suffices for life in Christ Jesus our Lord, to whom is due all glory for ever. Amen.